Under The Plow

eight years of columns for the Saint Albert *Gazette*

by

Paula Johanson

I0142612

UNDER THE PLOW

First edition. July 25, 2024.

ISBN: 978-1989966303

Written by Paula Johanson.

Table of Contents

"Then followed... years in limbo: a precarious job in industry, parttime teaching when I could find it, fellowships, editing...A broadening time. The experience of marginality is good for the soul and better for the intellect. And throughout, the joy of watching my children grow..."

Chandler Davis, "The Purge." *Tablet*, Oct 2, 2022. https://www.tabletmag.com/sections/history/articles/the-purge-chandler-davis

Introduction

I was a writer when we moved from Victoria to my spouse's parents' farm north of Edmonton. In addition to writing novels that got the *nicest* rejection letters ever, I wrote short stories and poems as well as book reviews and commentaries for newspapers and magazines. So it was natural that I would approach the local newspaper in Sturgeon County as a writer.

The editors at the *Gazette* turned me down, nicely enough that three years later I contacted them again. I'd written many stories and poems and articles and even another novel by then, but still had not had a novel accepted by a book publisher. My first nonfiction book, *No Parent Is An Island,* had just been accepted by a little press in Calgary, so that was terrific news worth sharing when I approached the local newspaper. But no, they didn't need me as a writer and didn't even run a review of my book.

I tried again three years later at the local newspaper, with added experience in the publishing industry as an editorial assistant. The *Gazette* editors turned me down again with a rejection letter nearly as nice as those sent by book publishers who turned down my novels. I kept on writing articles and reviews for radio and magazines and newspapers and books, and edited a couple anthologies of other people's stories.

Then one day a phone call came while I was writing interviews and profiles for a career guide from a publisher in Montreal. On the phone was the assistant editor for the local newspaper in Sturgeon County. "We want you to write a column for the *Gazette*," she said eagerly, and paused for my reply.

I laughed.

"No, you don't," I said.

"Yes, we do," she said, a little confused. She described how she'd heard my pieces on CBC Radio, and read my commentary "The Rooster" in *The Globe and Mail*, and found my book in the local library. "We would like you to send a resume and contact information for our files."

"No, you wouldn't," I said cheerfully. "Look in your correspondence files. Your office has received my letters of application with resumes on three separate occasions, and turned them down."

A pause. "We have?"

"You're new here, aren't you?" I said. "Your name has been on the masthead for only a few issues."

"I don't think you understand," the assistant editor said, a little unsteady but still trying to turn the conversation in the direction she expected. "The *Gazette* is asking you to write an opinion column for us."

"Well, isn't that nice," I said, which was close enough to an answer she expected so she could carry on to her next prepared statement.

"Your column will go on the page opposite the editorial and letters to the editor," she explained brightly. "You'll be one of our rotating series of writers for that spot. There are five of you, so you'll be in the paper almost every month!"

"Nice location on the Op-Ed page. Are you looking for a consistent number of column-inches, or under a thousand words?"

There was a pause while she audibly blinked, before saying slowly, "Keep it between seven hundred and fifty and nine hundred words, if you can."

"I can do that."

"And we will pay you, too – forty dollars a column!"

I couldn't help laughing again.

"Yes, we really will," she said brightly. "Excuse me?" she asked, unsteadied again by my chuckles.

"You're offering only forty dollars?"

"That's what we pay all our column writers," she said, a little bewildered.

"It's half the going rate. That piece of mine you mentioned, "The Rooster" – *The Globe and Mail* paid me a hundred and twenty for it."

"But they're the biggest paper in the country!" she protested. "And the back page of their first section is the most read page in Canada."

"And reading my piece there is why you want me to write for you."

"Forty dollars is what we pay our columnists. It's what we've always paid."

"It hasn't gone up in a while, has it?"

She paused, then rallied. "We'll put your name at the top of your column every time," she promised.

"Of course you will. It costs more if there's no by-line."

"Send us your photo, a nice close-up of your face, and we'll put it right by your name," she offered.

It was my turn to pause and stare unbelieving at the phone. "No, I don't want to get recognised when I go to town any more than I already am. No headshot."

"But some of our columnists really like having their photo in the paper," she wheedled.

"Two of them," I said. "And they're men who live in Morinville and Saint Albert. I live on a farm ten miles from the small town of Legal. I've already had one fan turn up at my farm un-expected, half a mile from the nearest neighbour."

"Oh." Then, in the most natural tone I'd heard from her so far, she said, "I can't pay you any more than fifty dollars a column when I'm paying the others forty."

"I'm not asking you to."

"You're ... not?"

"I'll write you three columns for forty dollars each," I said. "You go ahead and read them, print them, and see what response you get in the next while, like letters to the editor and such. People like what I write. If I mention a book, they go to the library and bookstore and ask for it. You get response, you'll start paying fifty dollars a column, but to all five of us columnists, not just me."

She agreed, and kept her word.

That's how I started writing columns for the *Gazette*. The editor had me send in extra pieces of writing, for spares to use when other columnists missed their deadlines. It got so that weekly paper had two columns of mine nearly every month. Though most readers lived in the city of Saint Albert or the town of Morinville (home of The World's Largest Toque), the paper served all of Sturgeon County. Farmland and acreages there were on quiet long dusty gravel roads and dark at night under the stars. The Big Dipper – called The Plow in England – wheeled in the northern sky, and the aurora borealis danced overhead, low enough to move when my spouse taught me to whistle at them.

Phone

Name one electric appliance that is in almost every home in Canada. You'll be wrong. No, it's not the television! There's an average of two of those in most Canadian households—at least for those people who want the jabbery things around.

No, the jabbery electric appliance I mean is the telephone. Not every home has one. Ten percent of Canadians have no phone.

I find life without a phone hard to imagine. That's even after our first summer on the farm, half a mile from the nearest phone. There was a certain freedom from tyranny in knowing the phone was not going to ring. There was also a certain feeling that our children were sure to fall out of poplar trees and break their necks. I didn't ever want to run half a mile to my in-laws' place to call an ambulance. So we had a phone put in.

Easier said than done.

We made the call and were told the phone company's truck would come to the farm next Wednesday. We gave the legal land description of the little white house: a mile north of the highway, south-east corner of the south-east quarter Section 56. Houses out here don't have numbers by the front doors. Houses out here don't even have stairs by the front door. Some of our neighbours don't even have front doors at all, just a place where a front door will be put some day. Our little white house is the only house out here where the front door gets used. It's the only door we have. But then we're odd. Our neighbours are sure we're odd because we use our front door and didn't use to have a phone.

And we didn't get one next Wednesday, either. Oh, we saw the phone company truck drive by several times without stopping. So the next day I hiked to my in-laws' place and called the phone company. They said their driver couldn't find the house.

This was hard to believe. There are only three houses on our stretch of road, of which one is both little and white. I promised to stand in our driveway with a large sign and they promised to come next Tuesday.

They didn't show up. Instead, the truck stopped at our neighbour's grey house. No one was home. So they broke into his house and forcibly installed a telephone.

Our neighbour didn't like this at all. He was just getting used to having a TV set in his tiny house, behind the back door. His house had only one door, like ours, but his was definitely a back door. Now he had a phone he didn't want. He didn't like anyone breaking in, either. The phone company apologised to all of us and promised to install our telephone next Thursday.

Thursday we flagged down the phone company truck as it passed. It didn't take long to have the phone installed. Before he left, the phone man carefully wrote the wrong phone number on our phone. He also left behind his screwdriver.

So next time we needed phone work done, my husband bought a book and all the wires and tools. He already had the screwdriver, eh? Then he installed our own new phone, right by the front door. Our only door.

The Rooster

My morning routine of farm life is endlessly the same, winter and summer: breakfast and morning chores – feed the pigs, chickens and guinea pigs – start every day, whether the kids are scrambling to catch the school bus or I'm heading out to the garden to pull weeds. But occasionally the routine is punctuated by excitement which can be under or out of my control.

"The rooster hit me!" seven-year-old Lila wailed one autumn morning, running back from the chicken yard with bleeding bruises on her hands and legs.

"Was it Cock-a-doodle-doo?" I asked, looking around for our big Barred Rock Rooster, whose comb stood almost as high as Lila's waist. He had rushed at the kids a few times the previous year, until we showed them how to "make themselves big," then yell at him.

"He never bothers me," Lila snuffled. "It was the little one." That one was a gaudy rooster given to us by the neighbours with the dairy farm. The strutting little bantam fought with the big rooster several times, before each settled down to patrol his own area of the chicken yard trees and brush, inside the chicken wire fence.

Before going to Victoria for ten months to take a Fine Furniture Making course, Bernie had checked the chicken yard fence and assured me that it was solid. "The coyotes won't bother getting in in the daytime," he told me. "Just close the birds all in the chicken house at night and they'll be fine."

I never worried about coyotes getting the chickens, especially once they were shut into the chicken house Bernie had made out of an old granary. (In fact, I envied the chickens their 10' by 10' shed and coveted one like it for a writing office!) I never worried about the coyotes bothering the children, either. The only coyotes we had seen ran at any sight or sound of humans. We told the twins that if a coyote came close, to "make themselves big" and yell, like with the roosters.

But now I worried about this rooster attacking the children. The bantam rooster weighed less than ten pounds, feathers and all, but he sported a pair of spurs as long and sharp as the Barred Rock rooster's own heavy armament. In addition, he appeared to have either a wicked temper or something to prove. Maybe being Number Two meant he tried harder.

Egg collecting time comes every morning, and when Lila's chatter to the laying hens broke off with yells and crying, I'd come running, clomping in my winter boots on the frosty ground. Ben came to her rescue too, but even together the twins couldn't hold off that feisty rooster.

"Dad showed us how to kick the rooster if he hurts us," Ben explained. I knew that trick too – slip a foot under the bird's breastbone and loft the squawking rooster high into the air. This disoriented our other roosters in the past, and calmed their attacking behaviours. But Feisty must have been part football, because he bounced back ready for a fight.

Don't ever close in for hand-to-hand combat with a rooster. Believe me, they are past masters at it, expert at darting and ducking and leaving an opponent bruised and cut with only a few feathers clutched in clenched jaws... excuse me, I did really get into the combat whole-heartedly. For this I went to University?

When Lila couldn't collect eggs without being attacked, Bernie had intervened to show the rooster who was boss. He caught that feisty rooster and carried him upside-down to where she was putting brown, white, blue and speckled eggs into her basket. Thoroughly limp, the dangling rooster submitted to her petting and chiding, and for a month he behaved much better.

But after Bernie had been gone a while, the rooster turned mean again. Nothing would stop this powerhouse with sharp beak and spurs.

So I ate him.

All right. That's a shameful admission for someone who is trying to be Vegetarian and gets away with it about 90% of the time. The latent Flower Child in me wants to live in peace with all creation. And as a teacher I try always to model co-operation and reconciliation.

But the gardener I am becoming knew exactly what the solution was, when to do it, and did it with confidence.

"That's the last time that feisty rooster will bother any of us," I told the kids as I washed my bleeding hands after shutting the chickens in for the night. "Tomorrow I'm going to put him in the stew pot."

The kids left on the school bus before I opened the chicken house door. (I found out later from Lisa, the bus driver, that they proudly announced, "Our Mom is gonna kill that rooster today!") The chickens were still groggy in the morning chill, but it took three rounds before I captured that little feisty rooster and held him upside-down by the feet. I let the others into the chicken yard and went back to the porch with my inverted enemy.

He was so much more placid hanging upside-down with his gaudy wings limp and his beady eyes staring blankly. If he could have stayed like that, I'd have kept him around for the winter.

Nothing doing. He gave all of us enough grief already. The last thing I needed while living alone with the kids on the farm in winter was to have to carry a rooster around by the feet whenever I did chores. You know, we never had days like these in suburbia or the inner city... Peaceful country life – Hah!

For the sake of animal lovers, I draw a curtain over Feisty's final moments. Suffice it to say that he never saw the machete when I took him behind the tool shed where a month earlier Bernie had killed chickens for me to pluck and clean.

It was ever so much easier to do only one chicken, instead of a freezer full. The pigs didn't get as much of a treat in their trough though, as they began playing the Happy Snake Game with the intestines. Soon I was putting into my slow cooker something that could have come nicely wrapped in plastic from a supermarket. Seven hours of simmering yielded a fine chicken stew when the kids came home.

The news on the school bus the next day was: "Our mom made ROOSTER STEW for dinner last night!" It was also the news at the school and the mail box and the store in town. The legend grows.

Orwell

I was pregnant in 1984, and now my daughter is studying George Orwell.

Orwell wrote a lot more than the novel 1984, but that's the one people remember best, and it's the one studied in schools. These days, if you've read anything political, or sociological, you've read 1984. It's one of the classics in our brave new world.

It's worth re-reading, which I've been doing inbetween back-to-school shopping and putting what harvest I can glean from our garden into Mason jars and the freezer. Oh, that and reading newspapers and Internet news services. It strange to read the novel of Winston Smith earnestly re-writing old press releases so that the enemies mentioned conform with the current Enemy of the State, and then turn to actual news stories from far away. Who is the real-life Enemy of the State this month? Is it a cowering figurehead, or one who stockpiles weapons? Is it the government leaders who oppress and starve their own citizens, or the prisoners held without trial by a democracy? And are they enemies of our state, or our state of mind?

I find it even more unsettling to read the news from closer to home. It's always a lot easier to believe that a time of war will not destroy everything, once the harvest comes in. But the harvest isn't bringing good news this year, except about the sharing that some people are doing. My friend's Arabian horses will be boarded by a generous man, so that these gentle, imperial animals will not starve or be shot for dog meat. I thought about that while turning the pages of 1984. No animals appear in that bleak, totalitarian novel. There is no room for anything but the State.

At least our own government is sending experts from Winnipeg to Europe, where the Elbe River is flooding. The Great Flood in Manitoba was a reminder to us all, like the Ice Storms back East and the Blizzard of '98 in Victoria, that there are great deeds to be done by soldiers and civilians alike in disasters. Heroes do not need to take up arms against our fellow humans to be heroes.

"The essential act of war is destruction, not necessarily of human lives, but of the products of human labour," says Orwell. "War is a way of shattering to pieces materials which might otherwise be used to make the masses too comfortable, and hence, in the long run, too intelligent. Even when weapons of war are not actually destroyed, their manufacture is still a convenient way of expending labour power without producing anything that can be consumed...." If that angered me half as immediately as the housefly which persists in landing on my right arm, I should summon up the resolve to remove War from the world as effectively as I have dealt with the housefly.

It's hard to solve all the world's problems, but I wonder just how much War would go on if everyone had a full belly and a safe home, as I do here in Canada, even in a year of lean harvest. I wonder how much fighting and terrorism is caused by greed and hatred, and how much is due to hunger and insecurity which are more easily cured. I've read some sociology texts and political works; pretty dry stuff in general. Far more accessible is Orwell's novel, or one of the movies based on it. The newer film version of 1984 was filmed in England in the late weeks of August, 1984, just the time Orwell set his novel, which was as much about 1948 and the aftermath of World War I and II as it was about Orwell's beliefs on sociology, politics and the future.

And now, in the late weeks of August 2002 when the children born in 1984 are old enough to vote and to serve in our Armed Forces, it really is time to look seriously into issues of war and wealth, peace and prosperity, and ignorance and strength. We can look in the national newspapers or in novels to see greed and dominance, but we will have to look into our hearts to find the confidence and industry needed by all people.

Knit

"Who are you making that for?"

I looked up from the laundromat counter, where my knitting was laid out, and saw the laundromat owner coming from her office. "That looks real pretty," she said. "What are you making?"

I smoothed out the knitting, showing the stripes of pale green and varied baby-soft colours, with a heart in the biggest stripe. "I'm making it for the Knit-In Protest for the G8 Summit. It'll be a little baby blanket when it's done."

"For the G8 Summit?" she asked, confused.

"Oh yeah. There are a lot of people who want to protest the G8, but aren't allowed to go into Kananaskis with the journalists. Some can't go to Calgary, either, so this is one of the alternatives that some people are doing." I explained that during the G8, there are people knitting as part of the Knit-In Protest, wherever they are. Instead of a march or a sit-in, this is supposed to be a personal act, for people who aren't comfortable with some of the more showy or aggressive ways of demonstrating.

"It's a protest?" She seemed to be warming to the idea of this non-threatening protest, that couldn't scare anybody. It might even be a little more productive than just marching – there'd be all these knitted projects to show for it when it's done.

The Knit-In Protest is not the only alternate demonstration. One band of demonstrators coming to Calgary from the USA were told by Canada Customs that they could not bring their costumes (with big paper machee heads) over the border. No costumes? For a peaceful gathering to protest The GAP store's overseas work conditions?

11

No Costumes became the new plan for that demonstration: the organizers did their protest naked, which strikes me as a peaceable, sensible alternative to pushing and shouting. Wearing tiny G-strings certainly beat the heck out of wearing black masks or riot gear. And the police responded just as peaceably and sensibly.

I had thought that since I was unable to get a press pass to Kananaskis, or afford the time away from my market garden, that I'd be unable to participate at all in the G8 Summit. But then I learned of the Knit-In, and resolved to participate. Out came my knitting needles and some baby-fine yarn from my closet, and I began work on a simple little blanket.

It's not a complex project, just simple purling rows and knitting rows. It won't change the world, but then neither does saying a rosary or meditating or reading a newspaper. What can change the world, though, are the thoughts we have while praying or meditating or studying – and the actions we take because of those thoughts.

Taking the time to knit a simple baby blanket is not as practical as buying a machine-made blanket, but it put my spare time in a laundromat to some use. It got me talking with another person about peaceful ways to express opinions about government policies. And that can't be a waste of time.

Tolkien

Lately I've been taking breaks from news reports in the papers and on radio and television, to read books or watch films. I've often wondered where art comes from – great art, popular art, classic works and modern entertainment. *The Lord of the Rings* is a film that's getting a lot of attention, even with only two of the three parts released so far. The screenplay went through countless re-writes, each time becoming more like the book it was based upon, a best-selling book by J.R.R. Tolkien.

Successful works of art seem seamless. It's hard to see the innumerable tiny movements of pen or brush that go into a painting or the training of a painter. There's a photograph of the artist Picasso in an old issue of the *National Geographic* magazine, a photo that shows the stocky man holding a small penlight in a dimly-lit studio. As the photographer held the camera's lens open, Picasso drew the outline of a minotaur, tracing it in the air with his penlight. It took a second or so to draw, but all Picasso's years of study to move his hand.

Tolkien wrote his most famous book, *The Lord of the Rings*, on request after the success of his earlier novel *The Hobbit*. Many authors would have rattled off a sequel much like the first, or perhaps a series which gradually takes the hero through a progression of adventures. Tolkien took seventeen years before he was ready to send "another hobbit book" to his editor.

He was right not to rush things. I've read some excerpts from the first drafts, and it's clear that early on in the writing of this novel, Tolkien had no idea where he was going. Characters introduced in the first draft disappear in a re-write. Dialogue is stiff and clumsy. The very first appearance of a Black Rider changes the story completely. The image of a hobbit and the wizard Gandalf riding a horse is cut from the opening chapters, only to appear much later – with a different hobbit, a different horse and even the wizard is much changed by that point in the story.

As he wrote the early chapters, Tolkien sent most of them to his son Christopher who was then fighting in France in the Second World War. While Christopher was facing his real-life challenges, J.R.R. was stuck with his hobbits and Strider in the village of Bree. At the time he had no idea of who Strider was, or why Gandalf had failed to meet them there.

Some readers think that the gathering shadows of danger as the story moves on, and the horrors of battle and death, are a metaphor for the war that took place while the book was being written. But the author insisted this was not so: he had not written an allegory of Hitler or the war that seemed so necessary that even some Quakers volunteered for alternate service.

He did admit to a father's worries for his son, and a veteran's worries for his fellow servicemen and women. Tolkien had fought in the First World War, a generation earlier. It was shattering to experience war at a scale that killed more men than all the battles during the previous hundred years combined. From poison gases to croplands made barren, these are images that were the source of the story of hobbits barefoot in the wilderness, and the return of a King who brings unity and defense.

Tolkien lost all his closest friends, all fine young scholars and athletes, in what was called the Great War. So it is understandable that he could later write this book in which a team of talented companions try to save the world, and all survive – except for the one who was too proud to believe he could be tempted by great power.

It is not an easy book to read, in these days when news of war in a far-off dry land comes even to our own dry cropland. It is not an easy film to watch when shattered bodies can be seen on television without any special effects make-up or rubber masks. Works of art are metaphorical – or not – and can be re-written or revised as an artist approaches her or his vision. These days, works of art, like Picasso's *Guernica*, are sometimes even covered up when world leaders gather, lest the sight of them bring too many questions to mind. But we can still hope that in the works of our hands, and the works of our friends and neighbours both near and far away, great power does not have to corrupt our actions into great evil.

Complaint

Each day, there are things not worth complaining about, and things worth complaining about. The hard part is not the decision whether to complain, it's knowing who to complain TO.

An April blizzard sandwiched between two heat waves so unseasonably warm that I'm reaching for Popsicles in April? No complaint. The worst part for me was shovelling the driveway, unlike the 120 people whose vehicles went off the highway between Red Deer and Airdrie. And who would I complain to, anyway? Weather reporters aren't responsible for my snow tires. At any rate, the best part of the heat wave was learning that the nearest convenience store 14 km from my farm stocks Mr Freezes in April. Bliss!

It takes understanding emotions and their impact to know when to complain, about what, and to whom, and most sensitively – how. If my blood pressure rises and my palms get sweaty in the supermarket, it may indeed be time to ask the produce manager "Am I just grumpy today, or are produce prices really getting unreasonable?" This opening led to the produce manager agreeing with me that even seasonal produce, such as asparagus, simply costs an appalling amount.

My blood pressure and heart rate went up again at the check-out counter, when I discovered that the plastic rods used to separate each customer's purchases had been replaced – with new plastic dividers labelled with ads for a television news program. "It doesn't even say anything about your store or special sales," I said to the check-out clerk. "I know," she sighed. "But what are you going to do?"

What I did was go to Customer Service, and explain to the manager that ads on these dividers were aggressive marketing that offended me as a customer. If the ads had been for the United Way or other charities, I would have kept my pounding pulse to myself. But when stores sell my attention to news shows, they can learn to cope with getting my attention.

I've been paying attention to the news for weeks now, about the war in Iraq, learning things to complain about, and the names of people to whom I should complain. It's easy to find a Member of Parliament's address and phone number in the phone book. With computers, it's even easier to find @ddresses to send e-mail to Members of the Legislature and of Parliament. When I saw a newspaper photograph of a young boy whose arms had been blown off during the invasion of Iraq, I began typing e-mail letters, asking that Canadian resources be sent to help this child and others injured like him. But for my local MP – whose party leader won't rule out approving the use of nuclear weapons, who wouldn't carry my disapproval to his party leader – I'm writing a hand-written letter, with the child's photograph enclosed. And if my MP's face goes red or pale when looking at that photo, that's part of the reactions to expect when dealing with an invasion.

By contrast, a mere invasion of privacy is laughable. I got a good laugh the other day, reading the *Gazette*'s article about a local business that offers lie detector tests. The suggestion that employers make job applicants take these tests got me laughing so hard my sides ached. I'm looking for work, not as a police officer or child care worker or nurse, but the idea of taking a lie detector test when applying for any other kind of job is so unreal, it must be funny. If it's not funny, it's scary.

I'm sure that local business is someone trying to earn an honest living. But it would make me feel like the inventor of duct tape must feel about thieves who tape windows before breaking into houses.

Y'see, lie detectors measure the pulse, blood pressure, sweat, and breathing rate that I've been mentioning. A trained tester compares a person's measurements while the tester asks ordinary questions and sensitive questions. But a person who is already nervous can have sweaty palms or jittery pulse without lying. Trained testers make allowances for this. Still, I don't plan to let my honesty be questioned this way, when tests can be made invalid by something as simple as wearing shoes that pinch.

Maybe I'll end up taking the test anyway, just for fun. I can lower my blood pressure by 10 points in ten seconds – it's my party trick. It would be fun also to see the results if the roles were reversed. Far better than complaining.

So, I'm Going Deaf

One spring, my husband insisted I wasn't paying attention when he called, and my kids insisted that that they were NOT mumbling. Mostly to prove that I still had the hearing of a twelve-year-old child who never listens to Utah Saints, I went for a hearing test. That's how I learned I have a hearing loss in both ears.

The official diagnosis was Meniere's Disease. In plain English, that means "No head injury, no tumor... Damn if I know why the nerves aren't working." I got that diagnosis after being put on a nine-month waiting list to see an Ear Doctor, to find out whether I had the kind of tumor that comes with a nine-month life expectancy. There's nothing like the joy of telling my family about my brain scan. "Good news! They found my brain."

Five years earlier, I had unusually good hearing. Now, sounds have to be louder for me to hear, especially low sounds. It's been a couple years now since I heard the great horned owl in our windbreak trees, and my family has adjusted as much as I have. Mostly we try to keep our sense of humour.

There are special considerations for the teenaged members of a family when a parent becomes hard-of-hearing – more than just what to do when requests for your allowance go unheard. My teenagers have gracefully given me suggestions for young people who have a parent with a new hearing loss. These apply to parents of either gender, but the word "mother" is used, as fathers are notoriously able at the best of times to avoid responding to sounds generated by their teenaged offspring.

Good News: You can now play your music Really Loud, especially in your room with the door closed. Use speakers instead of headphones, of course.

Bad News: You are not going to get away with using bad language around your mother. Her hearing may not be good anymore, but her "parent radar" is probably working fine.

Tech News:

-A telephone with a volume control can be turned up by your mother. Get used to turning it down every time you pick up the receiver. Turn the ringer up loud, too. It may be annoyingly loud to you, but hey, your mom's not complaining about your music.

-Get a teakettle with an automatic off-switch for when it boils dry. Sell any other kettles at a yard sale, even if they have loud whistles, and keep the money.

-An answering machine takes messages. It does not miss the one important word or be unable to recognize someone's voice. Check for your mother's messages as well as your own – you may no longer be the last one to know her plans for a family outing.

Tech Support:

-You are now the Fire Alarm specialist. Test all smoke alarms, keep new batteries in them, and hold Fire Drills. You're the one able to hear an alarm and wake up, so this is your chance to be a dictator. Make the most of it.

-If your mother now has a hearing aid, buy spare batteries to keep in your wallet and in the car. When she needs a battery, give it to her and do the dance of joy. Your mom carried a diaper bag when you were little. This is a lot easier.

Social News:

-Tell your friends in the band Wizard that your garage is fine for rehearsals, even when your mom is home.

-When out with your mother, walk a step or so ahead of her rather than behind, if you don't want her continually turning round and round to find you or holding your hand as you walk through the mall.

-Other parents might bring junk food or shwack from work for their teenagers and friends. Your mother will hand out pairs of foam earplug hearing protectors.

-Get used to looking at your mother when you talk, and to repeating and re-wording what you say. Even so, she will still understand you better than during the two or three years you said "Waah!" whether you were hungry, messy, or had a boo-boo.

Ultimately, you'll find ways to adjust and adapt. You could even get a blinker switch from a string of Christmas lights and put it on the plug for the radio in the kitchen, then take bets from other family members on how long before your mom notices.

Speech

I hadn't realized how time catches up with everyone eventually, until I was asked to make a speech for my mother's Retirement Dinner. Surely Mom wasn't retiring yet from the Personnel Office in BC's Department of Highways. What would the office do without her? She was their star pitcher on the softball team! How would the office computers be re-organized next year? She was the one who told the systems analysts what the systems they were analyzing were actually meant to do.

But as Mom pointed out, she had been enjoying Fridays off for a couple of years now, since she worked flex-time hours. She was looking forward to organizing her own days to suit her own schedule. She had just bought a membership at the municipal golf course. She signed up for a soapstone-carving class taught by her daughter-in-law at the community college. Then, too, my mother's own parents were aging and needed more help to run their errands and get to all their appointments. And within two weeks of her retirement, she claimed she had no idea how she had ever got *anything* done when she was working. There was so much to be done!

But then, my mother has always organized whatever she was doing, with practical rules for success. She was an at-home mother for a few years when my brother and I were small, and even then she baby-sat other children, and ran summer programs in the playground.

When my mother began working outside the home again, after my brother Karl and I got big enough to be trusted to walk to school with our musical instruments and not to tie our after-school sitter to a stake in the yard, there were some new rules made around our family home. They had to do with phone calls.

Mom said: If we fell down after school, we could get a Band-aid from the babysitter, but we could also call her at work. If Karl took the last pop when it was my turn and he wouldn't clean up after the dog but I did it two times last – don't call. If the clothes dryer is filling the basement up with smoke, call at once – from the neighbour's phone.

And if the cat got into Dad's fishing tackle box and has a fish-hook through her cheek – call Dad.

These rules worked pretty well for a number of years. But during one long, cold winter on the farm in Alberta, trapped indoors with my kids in a snowstorm, I called Mom long distance to apologize for every bit of grief I ever gave her as a kid. Mom always knows what to say. "You were a joy to raise," she said. "You never gave us a moment's grief."

I knew even as she said it that there were plenty of moments when Karl and I swung bats and chair legs at each other's heads, or when she told me to go hose down my muddy brother on the driveway after football practice, or when she was awake doing laundry at midnight when I came home from the only drive-in movie I ever went to on a date.

But now there will have to be some new phone call rules for retired people so we won't give each other grief. I'm sure my brother Karl will agree on these phone call rules.

So listen up, Mom. When you're going to Palm Springs for three weeks, call so we know where you are. (If we're having a blizzard, we may hang up, but call anyway.) When you join a new fitness club, call so we know to give you track suits for Christmas. When you take up art or writing, call so we can admire your creative work.

And when you're cleaning out the basement and moving the furniture or appliances – call Karl.

Enjoy your retirement, Mom.

Planning

There is something I haven't heard said about the Kyoto Accord and its possible effect on Canadians. It takes planning ahead, to be able to do things without thinking about them.

I know, that sounds like a paradox. But ask anyone who has narrowly avoided a car collision, were the driving lessons worth it? Anyone who has helped an injured person knows that a First Aid course can be more than comfort, it can mean the difference between life and death. Even something as ordinary and simple as piecing together a patchwork quilt goes much easier if the quilter has gathered a complete sewing kit together and has put dinner in the slow cooker before starting work.

Planning and preparation enable us to know how to meet our goals. We can still learn as we go along, but a lot of untimely decision-making and dithering can be avoided.

I'm thinking about my son's friend Jay, who made himself a jumpsuit with zippers all over the sleeves and legs and torso. Jay didn't want any advice about how to fasten the bottom ends of the zippers, which he took from old jackets and sewed together. He wore the jumpsuit to a party in Edmonton, and on his way home Jay fell asleep on the LRT. He missed his station, and woke up at the end of the line. Jay jumped up to go find a pay phone and call for a ride – and that was when he learned about planning ahead.

While Jay had been asleep, someone had unzipped all his zippers. That was how he found himself standing in Clearview transit station wearing nothing but fishnet stockings with a pile of zippers at his feet.

There have been times during this drought that I've felt like that, looking into my dugout pond which is less than half-full. Did I plan ahead? I wonder what small part I have played in local and global climate change.

For weeks I've been looking at the gasoline pumps during fill-ups, thinking about a certain brand of premium advertised as having "20% fewer emissions." When the price of gas went down a few cents, I bought a tankful of premium for the price I'd been paying for regular. If I can justify using so much gasoline, I could try fuel that is less polluting. If each driver replaced one car trip a week with walking or taking the bus, there'd be that much less gasoline burned, and one more healthy walk. It's not much of a plan, but it's not rocket science – anyone can do it.

Over the last several years, we Canadians have shared in the general trends among industrialized nations which affect the world's climate. We are employed by and operating the same industries and services that feed and clothe and shelter us and maintain our health even as they use up phenomenal amounts of raw materials and create tons of wastes, some of it frighteningly toxic. Our industry is as unstable as Jay's zippered jumpsuit.

As a first step, we need to reduce our household use and waste of fossil fuel products and of electricity from fossil fueled power plants. It's a worthwhile plan, even though households consume less than 20% of fossil fuels, because then we can insist on the next step. Reducing domestic waste makes reducing commercial waste seem equally practical. Meeting the standards of the Kyoto Protocol only seems impractical to those who don't plan to clean up their own messes as a responsible cost of doing business.

The issue is not whether we need to meet the standards set out by the Kyoto Accord. We need to exceed them. These are standards of cleanliness and good business, for our own health and the climate of the world. We need to demand from ourselves, as workers and employers, the standards of efficiency and hygiene that we insist upon in our own homes. Simply by reducing inefficiency in fuel consumption, and by reducing the waste of recyclable or compostable trash, we can enjoy a comfortable standard of living. With a little planning, we don't have to end up like Jay, standing with a heap of zippers puddled around our feet in harsh weather.

Minivan

My family has been driving a minivan this winter, and I can understand why these useful vehicles are so popular. There are heaps of reasons to drive a minivan. First of all, it's big enough for me to drive home my spouse, kids, a friend, a French horn and the groceries in only one trip. It's the only vehicle I've ever driven big enough to put my purse and a box of tissues somewhere that isn't under the driver's elbow. It's also big enough to get into the back to reach the box of tissues when it slides under the back seat.

Heck, it's big enough to get into even with an expanding waistline and sore arms from a workout at the gym. No wonder so many middle-aged parents drive a minivan! But at the same time it's small enough to get into without needing to use ropes, a pulley and a team of Sherpas. This is important when I am so short that I need two steps and a handhold to climb into any vehicle large enough to accommodate my husband.

All in all, a minivan is a fuel-efficient way to move a reasonable number of people and a reasonable amount of cargo. It feels good to be driving an environmentally sensible vehicle. If it's not as fashionable and tough as an SUV, well, neither is it so counter-culture as a camperized VW van. And it uses less fossil fuels than either, even if it doesn't have the flash of an SUV or the cachet of a cross-country pilgrimage.

I've learned how to recognize that a minivan driver used to own a full-sized van. The usual give-away clue is the custom installation of second-hand side mirrors, wide rearview mirror, ladder and roofracks. The driver may reveal his or her past when s/he reaches for the gearshift, gritting teeth and bracing him/herself on the steering wheel of the new automatic. Another clue is if the old handmade bumper sticker that used to read "Dont laff yer dotter is riding with me" has been corrected. The bumper sticker now reads: "Don't laugh, your daughter is riding with mine to soccer practise."

Most minivans are full of kids. We got ours second-hand from friends with two small children, who understandably preferred going hiking over cleaning the vehicle. We took it through an automated car wash the first week we drove it, and gave our teenagers some rags, a pail of water and a bottle of ArmorAll to do the inside. The results were astonishing, and paid off big time.

It's easier to tell ours from all the other minivans in a parking lot, because it's dark blue instead of "back road brown." The roof is now an inch lower, so we can now park the minivan anywhere in a parkade without worrying about 6 foot clearance. The dark brown interior turned out to be pale gray under a patina of small fingerprints. The tarry dashboard proved to have a double cup holder full of ancient coffee. And while vacuuming out the back, my son found $2.57 among the sand and gravel, plus a Barbie doll head that he has sewed onto one of his punk jackets (next to the badge that reads: "Never Apologize for Your Art"). The minivan now has better fuel economy, after clearing out the gravel and improving the wind resistance.

I find a minivan is worth maintaining mechanically as well. There's lots of room in it for booster cables, spare battery, headlight bulbs and bottles of motor oil, transmission fluid, gas line antifreeze and windshield washer fluid. It's a lot more embarrassing to have car trouble when driving not only my own teenagers, but their friends as well, to the $2 movie theatre. And ultimately it's easier to keep the minivan tuned up than to have it towed and find some way to get home to the farm with the groceries, four baskets of laundry, a bag of library books and three 50 pound bags of chicken feed.

Yes, it's official. I have Minivan Mania. But there are also reasons not to drive a minivan anymore. It's hard to find your travel mug when it rolls away into the back. Stop at any school crosswalk, and four kids will get in and buckle up before they realize that you're not the parent of any of them. The drivers of SUVs don't bother to signal when changing lanes beside you, they'll just look down and laugh. (Remember at the gas station to smile at the SUV drivers filling their gas-guzzlers' tanks!)

But when the bumper sticker that says "My other car is a Triumph Spitfire" just isn't enough for me anymore, it'll be time to move on. I'll sell the old minivan to a fixer who can do his own transmission work, and I won't look back.

(Paula Johanson is willing to tell the story of towing the minivan twenty miles through ice fog to anyone making contributions toward her "New Bearing for My Minivan" campaign.)

Parking Lot

Now that we're into the New Year, I am proud to say I broke last year's resolution only four times. That resolution was: during the entire month of December not to enter a shopping mall. (Okay, not much of a resolution, but I nearly made it. And two of those four times were only to pick up library books on hold.) If a store had a door that opened to a mall, I didn't go there. My New Year's Resolution may be to avoid retail parking lots entirely, and one lot in particular.

The parking lot at Namao Centre is worthy of a Di Castri award for design. John Di Castri was the architect who designed the student residences at the University of Alberta. His buildings are easily identifiable: they look interesting, but people get frustrated and lost.

Namao Centre does look interesting, and there are a number of fine businesses there. But getting from point A to point B in that parking lot is an unspeakable headache. It's not just that parking improves once snow covers the painted lines, allowing drivers to park far enough apart that car doors can actually be opened. Nor are the stop signs scattered throughout the parking lot a problem. It's the traffic flow that is difficult to navigate. Should I turn right at a sharp angle here at the stop sign, or continue straight on forty feet to the four-way stop at a blind corner? Is anything easy there at all?

I've been inventing punishments for the un-named architect of Namao Centre and its parking lot. This wishful thinking takes the form of sentencing the architect to drive through Namao Centre. Doesn't sound very grim, does it? Well, wandering back and forth, looking for the way to a far corner of the lot while avoiding imminent collision is pretty grim. Now imagine the architect has a toddler, a seven-year-old child and a medium size dog, and all of them have to go to the bathroom. I defy anybody to find a parking place where the dog can be walked and a restroom can be found for the humans before one of the children – or the adult – is crying.

On days when I find myself taking a roundabout route through traffic approaching at random angles, I imagine that the architect's kids are hungry, and the architect has a cold.

On days when I'm really frustrated, I imagine that the architect hasn't had a cup of coffee yet, but is clutching two coats for drycleaning, a prescription for eczema, a grocery list and a note from the architect's spouse reminding them to be home in an hour with a bottle of Merlot to take to a potluck dinner at a friend's house in Mill Woods – and to please pick up a present to bring for the friend's birthday.

Of course, every time I imagine the architect's struggles I always insist that his or her wallet is empty of money, except for a bank card and a deposit envelope for which they must get a bank receipt. As for the car, it's a Dodge Caravan overdue for an oil change and the gas tank is nearly empty. And should the architect simply leave the vehicle and tromp around the parking lot on foot to complete all these errands, I insist that the weather must be rain, after a snowfall.

My sister-in-law does a lot of errands there. She likes this scenario, but says that the architect should also pick up a video for the babysitter.

The architect's imaginary struggles are so entertaining, I'm writing them up as a Role-Playing Game like Dungeons and Dragons. To play this game, the heroes have no swords or magic rings, just waterproof shoes and good peripheral vision. Any player who jumps up and down and shrieks either "Footpaths! There must be safe, dry footpaths!" or "I couldn't back out of here in an Austin Mini!" is awarded fifty bonus points. And the player who declares that all intersections must be set at right angles wins the game, and is allowed to re-draw the map of the parking lot. Hey, in fantasy games, people are allowed to win.

Coveralls

I am becoming a serious gardener. My first garden was small: just one spaghetti squash under a rhododendron bush. Now my family works acres of market garden. That sounds like serious gardening – but you can tell I'm a serious gardener because I wear coveralls.

People who are serious about this kind of work wear coveralls. Oh, it's okay to wear jeans and shirts sometimes. But if you wear jeans for gardening or fixing tractors, it's hard to get them clean enough to wear anywhere else. Coveralls are different. Nobody wears them anywhere else, so it doesn't matter if the knees are permanently stained, and motor oil dots across the front and one leg. Coveralls just have to have the old dirt beaten off and the old sweat washed out. Tears can be sewn or patched with any old stuff from the ragbag. And it doesn't matter if coveralls don't fit.

I had the hardest time buying my first pair of coveralls. They're normally sized for men with big shoulders. I'm not the shape of a man with big shoulders. By the time I found coveralls that fit me around the hips, the sleeves hung over my hands and the cuffs turned up as high as my knees. But I hemmed them and put them to good use for four years.

That taught me a reason for wearing coveralls instead of just shorts and a halter top in the summertime. The green dye faded over the summers till the back was burnt white. If that had been my bare back, well, with my pale skin I'd be a candidate for skin cancer now. As it is, on my face, neck and hands I use a sunblock with sun protection factor 45. That's almost as good a block as a flannel shirt.

There's another reason for not gardening in shorts and a halter top: mosquitoes get pretty hungry around here in June and July. I hear black flies get ferocious in some places. With long sleeves and pant legs, I only have to put bug repellent on my face and neck and hands and ankles. Considering what goes into bug repellent, I avoid it as much as possible. Want to bet that in ten years we'll be hearing the problems with mixing bug repellent and sunblock? It already makes me shiny, slimy and sticky.

This spring I picked up a new-ish pair of coveralls at a garage sale for five bucks. Okay, they weren't green this time. They're bright orange. But at least it only took an hour with the sewing machine to make them fit me. And that beats the heck out of paying forty bucks for a brand new pair. And now, I'll never be lost out in a field of beans.

The only problem is dirt and oil stains show on the orange, even when I wash them. One of the rules about serious gardening is Wear Clean Clothes. It's not about dirt – you can beat that off with a stick. It's not about offending your fellow gardeners – though if you wear hummy clothes no one will want to work near you. That's not just because you'll offend their noses. It's because you'll attract mosquitos. Those bloodsuckers siphon out your blood till you're a quart low. And no amount of bug repellent overcomes the bug attractant in your sweaty clothes.

There's no reason to clog up a washing machine with sand and oil from your coveralls. Beat 'em with a stick and thrash 'em around in a pail of soapy water, rinse 'em off with the hose and hang 'em on the line. They'll be dry for morning. Coveralls are good that way, unlike the rest of the laundry, which has to be sorted for colour, what it's made of, and how dirty it got. The rest of the laundry is easy to put off until there's nothing to wear. At that point desperate measures are called for.

Which is how I've become the only farmer around here to wear an underwire bra and lacey panties under my coveralls. At least, I assume I'm the only one. About ten miles away, I know someone named Wendy who farms a market garden with her own husband. But you know, I've never asked her if laundry day found her with nothing else to wear under her coveralls but her lacey stuff. And I can't see asking any of the other farmers. They're all serious farmers. Too serious for questions like that, at any rate.

Wood

My husband, the wood-worker. Excuse me, the fine furniture maker. He can look at a piece of lumber and tell you its name, the country it came from, and what it's good for making, from chairs to decorative inlay.

But he's still learning to identify trees. (Out in the park he will tentatively point at a Douglas fir next to a rhododendron bush and say, "The big one's the tree, right?") When we go hiking, he points out the softwoods. I show him the flat-needled Grand Fir, the bent crown of hemlock, and how one Douglas fir stump near a healthy tree will scab over with new bark. He's able now to identify cedar, at least, but I think that's because the distinctive scent of the green branches is like that of the milled lumber.

It's milled lumber that my partner knows best, and he can take me along a row of stacked boards, naming each by type and place. "Honduras mahogany, Philippine mahogany, padeuk, zebrawood, African purple heart," he says, and the names and textures are as foreign and exciting as Indian sandalwood.

He ran his hands along one board in a stack, smelled the dusty, arid scent of the kiln-dried wood, and admired the straight grain. "I'd like to get about ten dollars worth of this," he said aloud, as he turned away.

"You just did," I answered, checking the price tag.

But that was some time ago. Prices are higher now.

Bernie brought several board-feet of a particularly nice kind of wood into the living room one afternoon. "Once I saw it, I had to have it," he said excitedly. "So I wanted to have it cut for me, and I had to find out how much it was in the first place. Finally I found the guy, the ...um..."

"The wood pimp," I supplied, the word 'salesclerk' having escaped him.

"Yeah," he admitted. "It does feel that way. But isn't it pretty? Look at that grain!"

Wood is not such a sordid font of carnal desires all the time, though. When Bernie and a friend went to the lumber yard one morning, they took our son Ben along. While the men walked between rows of stacked lumber, talking quietly to each other as they pointed out this piece or that price, Ben ran galumphing back and forth.

"He hasn't been in church before, has he?" asked the friend.

It took Bernie a moment to realize that, yes, they were in the wood church – and yes, Ben was behaving about like any kid does after half-an-hour sitting on a frustratingly hard wooden pew.

Wood has been a source of frustration as much as satisfaction for Bernie, I'm sure, from the fabulous foreign woods (so fabulously expensive, alas), to the mundane disappointments of a real-world workshop. Such as:

The project that splinters apart after hours of work.

The realization that a #5 wood plane just isn't the size needed.

Finding a piece of his black walnut plywood that had been set aside for making a cabinet now has six propeller fins for lawn ornament whirligigs drawn on it by the eighty-seven-year-old great-grandfather who also uses the workshop.

But there are triumphs too. There is the success of getting his furniture in shows by the Woodworkers' Guild or in an Art Gallery. He keeps a photo album of all his pieces. Mad cackles of glee will come out of the workshop when Bernie has set up a new jig – and it works perfectly.

The triumph I remember best is when both twins had an assignment to build home-made musical instruments. Their models were flimsy, but served well as patterns so they could show their dad what they wanted to do. Before that weekend day was through, Lila had a "harpagonical" complete with strings and tuning pegs, and Ben had something half like a mandolin and half like a dulcimer.

The twangs and plunks from these instruments were music to the twins' ears. How many kids got real wood instruments they made with their dads? The satisfaction of these home-made projects probably exceeded anything else Bernie has yet built. But I wouldn't count on that record lasting for long. There are two mahogany desks-to-be lying in pieces, and at least one is due for a writer who spends hours a day at a word processor...

Mad Cow

Well, I've been putting it off for weeks now. But there's no getting away from the news of the Lone Mad Cow. Over the last few weeks, even my own opinions on the Lone Mad Cow, and the whole issue of spongiform encephalopathy, have been solicited by several loyal readers of my words. And so, I turn at last to a topic I've been avoiding.

It's a rather heady experience, to be consulted. Pardon me for a moment, while I bask in the glow. All right, I'm back.

Before I state any opinions on the Lone Mad Cow, there's a confession that I have to make. I used to be ... a vegetarian.

I also own a tie-dyed t-shirt. But eating vegetarian for a few years had little to do with any "hippie" beliefs and lots to do with learning about factory farming and big meat packers. I had no problems with eating meat, but big problems with some animals being raised in conditions that are heartlessly cruel. It doesn't help, either, that some big slaughterhouses are torture scenes and the meat is often not inspected thoroughly enough to meet the federal inspectors' own standards for their own tables.

For my family, moving to the farm a dozen years ago was a big change. My family now raises vegetables and animals for our table. Experience is a great teacher. We learned how to raise animals, and butcher them for meat. We made friends with neighbours who keep cattle, or sheep or a dairy farm. And we've come to know three professional butchers who work at a small enough scale to treat the animals humanely and inspect the meat thoroughly. But some days, even now, I cook a vegetarian meal.

I did some reading about mad cow disease and spongiform encephalopathy in any animals, not just cows. Turns out that it's a brain protein problem: a protein molecule kinks up and can't do its proper job in the brain anymore. This kinked protein is called a prion. About one in a million brains – animal or human – just have this happen, for no obvious reason. That may be what happened to the Lone Mad Cow. The prion slowly kinks up other brain proteins. Most animals don't live long enough to have their brains be badly affected, especially food animals. Most of the prions stay in the brain and nerves.

If an animal with a prion is fed to the same kind of animals, the prion can spread. It might spread to other kinds of animals or humans. Prions are not easy to kill or clean up like a germ, so it's important not to let that one in a million disease spread. So, I've come to hold the following opinions – as personal opinions.

I think it's all right to eat animals, if we treat them considerately, not cruelly. Humans evolved to eat some meat, and lots of plant foods. We don't eat sick animals.

I think it's best if our animals eat their natural food, and get to that natural food by walking around. Free-range, grazing animals taste good to me. I can understand bringing hay or grain – real food – to animals that are kept in a field or paddock too small to support them by grazing.

But when animals don't get enough real food, and are fed "supplements" made from ground-up animal parts, that's just not right. That's how Britain had so many cows with spongiform encephalopathy a few years ago. There were too many cattle and not enough grass and hay, so their cattle were being fed straw and ground-up downers, dying sheep and cattle, for a protein supplement. Before long, some of the downers turned out to have prions. That's why in Canada, we don't feed our food animals "supplements" made from animal parts.

Anyone who is worried about mad cow disease, or about the problems of big meat-packing plants, would do well to contact a small butcher or meat packer or look in the Want Ads. Buy a young steer or a lamb or turkeys from a farmer. Pick up the neat packages and put 'em in your freezer with confidence. This plan beats worrying about a one in a million problem – and it won't stop you from learning a few tasty, healthy vegetarian recipes as well.

Car

Have you seen this comedy sketch from the TV show Kids in the Hall? Comedian Scott Thompson puts a picnic basket in a car, then tries to start the engine. It won't start. He adjusts the sunvisor, wipers, and radio, but the car still won't start. He opens the hood, looks around without touching anything, then tries again. He gives the car a swift kick, but that doesn't work, either. He takes the picnic basket out and says: "I should really walk to the picnic anyway. I'll just roll the car into the driveway to wash it." While rolling, the car starts (of course!), so he drives away cackling with glee.

It's not that people really believe cars are actually started by magic. It's that cars are influenced by factors that seem as arbitrary and nonsensical as magic. And it's not just the non-mechanics who notice this.

Mechanics tell me: "Never test-drive a used car on a rainy day. It'll run better than it does on a dry day. Humidity affects the compression." It's a great big hot engine! How could a few raindrops would make any difference? Apparently it does, I have learned. I'm still learning if compression in an engine is like the compression I feel under an armload of car owner's manuals.

Whoever invented the auto-delay switch on my car's headlights knob deserves to be smacked. Why install a sensor that automatically turns the headlights on in the dark? I can tell when it's dark! The gizmo shorts out for no obvious reason, and then if you turn on the headlights (without turning off the sensor) after a few minutes the headlights will cycle from low to high beams to parking lights to off, randomly, every few seconds. That's bad enough on city streets, and really scary on the Coquihalla Highway. Every mechanic I had service that car cussed that switch out and wished to replace it with an ordinary on-off knob. Why not? That's one of the things I don't understand about cars.

I used to drive an old Datsun hatchback that wouldn't start some winter afternoons until I waited twenty minutes and tried again. It wouldn't pull this trick at home, but only in parking lots near a Canadian Tire store. I carried booster cables and a second car battery around all one winter for moments like this until I realized that the deva of the car was shopping in CanTire and wasn't back yet. It was like having another husband wandering in the hardware store.

I drove that quirky Datsun for another year until the clutch went CLUNK at the mailbox and wouldn't engage or dis-engage the gears. No big problem if the mailbox had been at the end of my driveway. Unfortunately, the mailbox was in my neighbour's driveway, a mile from my farm. And it was winter, and my mother was in the car.

My mother was already worried about me living on an isolated farm. Picking her up at the airport in an ancient beater hadn't helped. Now that the beater was clutch-less, this was clearly a disaster. First, she thought we'd freeze to death, walking a mile in the snow. Then, when I backed the Datsun out of my neighbour's driveway onto the highway and turned the motor off, she thought we'd get hit by another vehicle. (I'd already looked for any traffic.) She watched me move the gearshift to first and start the motor. "How are we going to get home in first gear?" she wondered.

"Synchromesh," I said, like a magic word. I smoothly accelerated and shifted the Datsun into second when the sound of the engine was right. Second gear was enough to get us off the highway and down a gravel road to the farm. That worn-out Datsun never moved again, and was towed away to a scrapyard.

My mother is confident that I can handle any vehicle, all because I knew the word "synchromesh" at the right moment. I haven't told her yet that I picked up that word years ago, when my brother and I were learning to drive her own Datsun hatchback. Back then, clutches didn't seem so necessary if one just listened carefully to the motor... but I'm sure that experiments with gears are part of what starts a car on the decline to become a beater, giving it those little quirks that work, or don't work, like magic.

Peanut Butter

More than 78% of Canadians eat peanut butter at breakfast. At least, that's according to a recent survey by Ipsos-Reid commissioned by Kraft Peanut Butter. But which peanut butter is the best? I investigated that sticky question for CBC Radio, and had a lot of fun investigating why I eat one spread instead of another.

At my farmhouse, we use peanut butter three ways: on toast, in cookies, and another way I'll tell you about later. Usually I buy whatever "old-fashioned variety" of peanut butter is on sale at the grocery store, one with no salt, sugar or oil added. But there's a lot more choice on the grocery shelves than I've ever investigated. It's enough to make me rant out loud in the grocery store aisle, just like one character on an old BBC television comedy: "I don't want more choices, I just want nicer things!"

Was my family eating the nicest spread – or at least the one we liked the best – on our toast? I thought this was worth looking into. And so did the Saturday afternoon show on CBC Radio, Definitely Not The Opera. That's how my family's eating habits were broadcast nationally on a show that usually covers popular music and cultural trends.

For my investigation, I prepared three samples for a taste-test. I had organic peanut butter, President's Choice peanut butter, and some homegrown No-Nuts Golden Peabutter. We wanted to try a very Canadian and very local product. It's made and packaged in Legal, Alberta, using yellow peas instead of peanuts. The makers, Mountain Meadows Food Processing, believe that many people who are allergic to peanuts would not be allergic to their product.

Then I rounded up a focus group. That's a fancy marketing term for my daughter and a friend of hers, my son, and my niece and two nephews. All of these kids have eaten peanut butter since they were toddlers, though one of them announced to my distress that he doesn't really like it.

But I put out a set of samples for him as well as the other kids. We started with the first set of samples: peanut butter cookies. Everybody took three cookies, one of each kind, and solemnly chewed. Some liked one kind of cookie, some liked another, and for each of the three samples there was someone who liked that kind best. Interesting! And nobody was able to guess which cookies were made with which spread.

Then I brought out the second set of samples: peanut butter on toast. This time the kids' expressions were more thoughtful. Even though they thought they knew all about peanut butter-type spreads, it was funny to see their surprise at how different each of the three samples tasted.

Well, the kids gave me plenty of reactions to use for my investigation for CBC Radio. And one of them ran shrieking when he learned which brand he'd chosen as his favourite. But there was still one more way we use peanut butter at my house. We use it to bait mouse traps.

Hey, we tried using cheese, but the mice nibble it off without triggering the trap. But a dab of sticky peanut butter gets a mouse tugging until... SNAP!

So for my investigation I got four new mouse traps, and each got a dab of organic peanut butter, or President's Choice brand, or No-Nuts Golden Peabutter. One had no bait at all – that was our control for the test. I left each trap out in my porch overnight, to see if any mice took the bait.

The final verdict among my human focus group: for making cookies, a majority of our testers liked the organic peanut butter best. For putting on toast, we liked the organic best. We agreed that No-Nuts Golden Peabutter is better in cookies than on toast.

And for baiting mouse traps... well, the mice in my porch ate all the bait. But the only trap that actually caught a mouse was dabbed with organic peanut butter. Of course, this is only the opinion of my mice. Your experience may vary.

Linda

I was going to write this week about service. Service to others, service for hire, the kind of service that gets useful things done. But it was brought to my attention that in my last column I apparently didn't say enough positive things about NoNuts Golden Peabutter.

Well, that's easy to fix! It's easy to praise a good food made locally by a locally owned company, especially when it wins awards and can be baked into tasty cookies. Apparently the inventor was hoping to make brown peas into a version of hummous, but was happy to come up with this spread that's a good, non-allergenic substitute for peanut butter. I guess that's the kind of attitude that says, when life gives you lemons, make candied peel.

That attitude of getting useful things done is less common than we all need it to be. Service sometimes means doing what is needed. While looking at the armfuls of gifts and toys going out of the stores this season, I wander over to the Santas Anonymous boxes to see how many donations get made. Coats for Kids is putting out the call again this year. And as for Food Banks, they've become a community service relied on even by some people with jobs, not only people without any luck or opportunity.

Service can also be something given under contract. My friend Linda contracted some services the other day, when she bought a washing machine. She had to take an afternoon off work to be home when it was delivered and installed. The truck arrived at the end of the day. The driver wasn't happy about delivering the washer to the basement, but he got it down the stairs and turned to go.

"Wait a minute," Linda called. "It isn't installed."

He wouldn't roll the washer across the floor and connect the hoses and drain. He stared at her blankly. He phoned his boss and explained the situation, then handed Linda the phone. "So what's your problem?" the supervisor asked.

Eventually the supervisor acknowledged that it was possible someone might buy a washing machine, arrange for delivery and installation, and expect the wheels to be removed and the hoses hooked up. The driver hung up his phone with a snort. "You just take the hoses," he said. "And ... oh. You need a different kind of hose."

So Linda arranged for the purchase, delivery and installation of the different kind of hose. Three weeks later, after several trips to the laundromat, doing a hundred dollars' worth of laundry and teaching her children how to do homework on a Maytag during the spin cycle, Linda took another afternoon off work.

Once again, the truck showed up at the end of the day. Once again, she had to explain to a truck driver yes, she really had arranged to have the hose installed and the wheels taken off the washer. He did both, eventually, after some protests. But he didn't roll the washer over to the taps before taking off its wheels, and he didn't connect the hose from the taps to the washer. "You can handle that," he said. "Anyone can tighten a hose on a tap."

Even Linda could, after the first try which sent water spraying everywhere. And she got the drain hose in place, too, which wasn't nearly as hard as wrestling a washing machine across the basement floor. Linda didn't need this learning experience to teach her to handle her own problems. She can handle a canoe on a white-water river, or a portage over rough trails. She can handle a job, and a home, and her children just fine. Apparently, the service section of a major department store is a lot harder for her to handle than camping in grizzly bear country. But Linda has a lot of friends. Some of them can help with her plumbing or appliances. And none of them will ever buy an appliance from that store – ever.

That store doesn't have the kind of service we all need. It doesn't get useful things done. We all need the kind of attitude behind NoNuts Golden Peabutter, one that sees brown peas as an opportunity, not as a disappointing lack of green snow peas. The attitude that sees not a failed recipe for hummous, but a marketable one for nutty-tasting spread, is an attitude that provides good services in a stronger economy.

Resolution

It's the time of year where people make resolutions and try to implement plans for a new year. Plans, that is, for a year closer to the ideal that is dear to their hearts. I don't know if your plans include losing twenty pounds and doing something to help starving orphans in Africa, or if you read *The Globe and Mail*'s recent column offering "tips for a saner new year." But if you're anything like me, losing twenty pounds would be smart; those orphans aren't the only ones who need SOMEbody's help; and I need some tips that aren't all for Toronto office-executives with a monthly income like what I earned last year.

I dunno what I'm doing, reading Toronto's national newspaper when I write for the *Gazette*. My neighbours raise produce or animals. *The Globe & Mail*'s tips are all for corporate executives who have a jam-packed urban schedule. Apparently they should have breakfast meetings standing up, computerize all light switches, get a drycleaner that picks up and delivers, order takeout, stop gardening, make standing appointments for manicures and haircuts, take VIP cab service, rent a car and driver, fly by charter, hire a chef and a personal assistant to write thank-you letters and a concierge and a team of house-cleaners and a kid to shovel your walk and someone to drive visitors around. Oh, and have no e-mail @ddress.

Now, I'm no urban executive, just a writer who lives on a farm. I don't have a drycleaner or a standing appointment for manicures. The last manicure I had, I did myself standing up in a Morinville laundromat while my laundry tumbled there to save our farm's well water. At my last breakfast meeting, my husband was my chef and I made my son my personal assistant and ordered him to takeout the trash. And the only chauffeur around here is me, driving my daughter around.

But oddly enough, last year I did happen to implement one of these *Globe & Mail* tips. It was "stop gardening" – but that was only because of the drought. Come spring, I'll try again.

If anyone is looking for some "tips for a saner new year" that work in this neck of the woods, I can come up with a few. Some of these might even work in the metro Toronto area, but I don't mind that.

1. If you eat meat, buy some from local farmers – maybe turkeys, lamb or a side of beef – and vegetables too, while you're at it.
2. Whatever you eat, keep your dishes and kitchen table clean, and eat one meal a day at the table with everybody who lives in your home.
3. Keep stamped postcards in your fridge. Write a postcard when you look for a snack. Try to write at least one card a week instead of eating a snack.
4. If you worry too much about wars, terrorism or diseases, pick a charity (local or foreign) and give 'em money or some of your time.
5. Keep your vehicle or bike serviced and tuned up. It'll work better, be safer and last longer.
6. Carpool when you can, even if only for one or two trips a month.
7. Swap footrubs.
8. Go to a municipal council meeting. It'll hurt less than any dentist.
9. While you're at it, go to a dentist, too.
10. Do something kind for a neighbour.
11. Plant something: herb seeds, a tomato plant, a tree. Plant it in a park or give it away if you have to, to keep it alive, then don't worry about it.
12. Keep or get an e-mail @ddress, give it only to your closest friends and family, and get some bright kid to show you how to filter out most random spam like ads for Viagra. Check for e-mail no more than once every few days.
13. One day a week, turn off the lights, turn down the heat and go to bed an hour earlier than usual.
14. Do hire a kid to clear your snow. Maybe, like me, you have a very very long driveway, and then there's the footpath to consider. In that case the kid may well need a snowblower or small tractor, but hire the kid

anyway. Small-scale entrepreneurs need business opportunities too. The economy may trickle-down but it won't clear your snow just with the power of a strong dollar.

Oh, and one more suggestion for a saner new year: this year, be sure to vote.

Scent

Nothing makes memories like scent. Smells evoke a place, a time, a conversation, or a whole relationship. Marcel Proust wrote in *Remembrance of Things Past* about dipping a madeleine pastry into a cup of tea, biting into it and being transported in memory back to a forgotten moment from his childhood.

There are scents that for me that evoke times and places near our farm. I know the smell downwind from the gas flare at the bend in Highway 28, the flare that burns with a flame four feet high, day and night since I moved here thirteen years ago. I asked a friend who lives near it how long that flare's been burning. She doesn't know. It's been burning as long as she can remember.

Other downwind smells tell me where I am. The smoky plume from the alfalfa plant with its understandable smells of grassy compost. The odd plumes from the oil refinery plants east of Fort Saskatchewan, when the east wind blows with the scents of long, complex molecules with names so long and complex that people call them by their initials. And the simpler smells of the dairies and pig farms, where manure is spread on fields, and the sharp reek mellows into plowed earth and growing things. Smells can tell the time of year, and who is working, and the long-term consequences of what is being done.

One recent hot day I was driving with my teenagers. When we came up to a corner where we turn off one highway, we opened all the windows as I slowed the vehicle for the turn. When you drive without air conditioning, you learn tricks like this, to blow a minivan full of fresh air from time to time. You also learn not to drive at 100 km/h with the windows open because it will seriously reduce fuel efficiency.

"What's that smell?" my daughter asked.

"Maybe a skunk," I suggested. "But I don't see one." There was some brush and boggy land along the highway, behind a barbed-wire fence.

"Something *dead*," said my son as I signalled for the turn.

"*Really* dead," agreed my daughter.

"Something *big*," my son added as I slowed and began the turn.

"Dead cow," I said, and completed the turn. A gust of wind buffeted our minivan and we all gasped and choked. "*Exploded* dead cow! Close the windows! Augh!" And as we coughed and wept, and sped up the hill, trying to get upwind of that bog so we could open the windows again – memory struck.

There was a house, some few years ago. I watched it being built, beside a road. It was moderately large, and when I left my little old farmhouse, I'd drive by and note the building as it progressed. There was a basement, rooms for kids, and a finished garage. There was a gravel driveway and fenced paddock for cows, and a wooden deck and a couple of fruit trees. Looked like a nice place. They had a nice herd of cows, too, and a truck and a nice car, and a nice load of hay bales was delivered before the paint dried on their paddock fence. My kids were small then. One went to a birthday party at that newly built house, and mentioned afterward that the house was nicely finished inside, too.

A nice family lived there, but I found it hard to go by that house. Perhaps I suffered from the sin of envy. Certainly my own house and yard and animals were not so big and orderly.

Then one day there was a dead cow in their driveway. It was a shame – I wouldn't wish that on anyone, not even the cow.

A day later, a tarpaulin was wrapped around it, but there was no disguising what was in that bundle. Not with the cow's legs pointing out stiffly, parallel to the ground. Next time I went by, the legs were pointing higher, the next time higher. The legs rose gradually over a few days to point almost upright, hovered there for a day, then moved ominously lower.

The memory brought to me by the scent of an exploded dead cow is not a memory of death and decay, but of something equally foul. Envy. I had envied the fine, finished house. I had coveted their orderly possessions.

There was a certain inevitable fascination to watching this cow swelling. It burned away any envy I might have felt. It reminded me that everyone has misfortune of some kind, whether it shows or not. It settled any worry I might have about why my own yard wasn't orderly. No matter what I've done or left undone in my life, I've never had a dead cow lie in my driveway for two weeks. And no matter how well anyone else has his or her home and work together, one dead cow can be a problem that won't go away easily.

Unlike the mad cow currently still in the news, this particular dead cow disappeared without a trace one day. When I passed by, my neighbour was out walking along her fence line, and we waved at each other. We do that now, smile and say hi when the bus comes by to take my kids and hers to school together.

Happy Snake-Oil to You

I never know what to give anyone. The worst present I ever gave anyone was a couple of years ago for my brother-in-law's birthday. He's a lawyer who likes hockey. He already has an iron bar for "passing the bar" – har har har – given to him at a previous Silly Party. Another relative gave him a holder for his business cards, decorated with a little ambulance chased by a tiny lawyer. So, I'm pretty sure that he's had more than enough gag gifts about being a lawyer. As for his interest in hockey, well, he already has season tickets and every hockey thing he needs.

So I bought a box of chocolates. Everybody likes chocolates, right? Well, everybody except the uncle I once gave chocolates... the diabetic uncle. But this present wasn't just chocolates. I wrapped the box in a home-made snake-oil pamphlet printed with big, curvy letters and lots of exclamation points. It took me a while to write this snake-oil pamphlet, but the memory of late-night infomercials gave me some inspiration. The chocolate box wasn't the biggest or best or most nifty, but the snake-oil pamphlet looked pretty cool. And it said:

New AMAZING Substance! **Mm-Hmm!**

Four out of five speech therapists surveyed agree: "A must-have for everyone who uses speech at work, at home and at play!"

During your busy days, or in the comfort of your home, do you find yourself talking? Many people do. But it's hard to admit it when you have the heartbreak of finding yourself at a loss for words.

"It was awful, I guess," says one victim after his experience. "Like, I just stood there, eh? And she goes, 'So?' And like, I said nothing, eh?"

Who among us hasn't known the loss of speech to happen? We'd all like to be witty, charming, and Johnny-on-the-spot with marvellously appropriate comments at every turn in the conversations so essential to a word-filled world. But at one time or another we've all been put on the spot like this during a crucial conversation, groped for words and come up ... speechless.

"... !! ... " agrees another victim, nodding and gesturing aimlessly as her eyes take on the glassy stare of a deer on the road, caught in your high-beams at night.

Or worse yet, if you force words out at moments like that, you may find yourself saying something truly dreadful! You will have to eat your own words and even so, may never recover from the public disgrace. Some poor souls are reduced to the horrors of foot-in-mouth disease, to which none of us are immune.

BUT – never fear! There is a new product on the market now, to relieve your stress and anxiety at those dreadful moments when you have nothing to say. **Mm-Hmm** has no moving parts, no active ingredients and a completely spurious effect upon anyone caught at a loss for words. And it's available over the counter without prescriptions.

You might ask, "How can something so simple work for me?"

Mm-Hmm is easy to use! The next time you are talking with someone and find yourself not knowing what to say next, simply apply **Mm-Hmm** to your tongue and hold it there. The tasty experience will relieve your distress! And naturally, no one could be expected to speak around so large a confection.

This marvellous remedy is made of durable ingredients, providing a natural solution to your immediate problem; a single **Mm-Hmm** should last long enough for people around you to fill the silence with comments of their own. You will not need to do more than listen attentively.

By the time you have consumed the **Mm-Hmm** you will either know what you wish to say, or the conversation will be at an end. Perhaps the immediate vicinity will be struck by a large, flaming meteor. At any rate you will be off the hook.

Mm-Hmm has a second use, for extreme situations only. When someone else is talking, you may offer them one. There are no guaranteed results, but you can take your chances. Enjoy freedom from word-related stress today!

That was my first and last effort at writing snake-oil. You might understand now why I'm writing for a local newspaper instead of enjoying a prosperous career in advertising.

At any rate, the chocolate box and snake-oil pamphlet went over pretty well at the birthday party. At least, I think it did. A sense of humour can be a very individual thing, but my brother-in-law likes reading, so maybe that helped. Gee, I hope he likes chocolate. But how can I ask him? I never know what to say.

Voting

Being ready takes a lot of preparation. Sometimes mental preparation is needed, sometimes research, and sometimes there are things that have to be done. But it's hard to be ready for my teenagers being old enough to vote in the next election. Does this mean I'm so old now that I have to take a couple of steps to the right along the political spectrum? It makes me wonder...

The other day my daughter came to me. "Mom? I have something to tell you."

"Okay, honey." I tried to prepare myself mentally for anything. But what could she possibly say? She's a good kid. "What is it?"

"I've been looking into the policies of the federal Liberal party." She hesitated. "And I – I agree with some of them."

"Of course you do," I told her. "Big party like that, been around a long time. It'd be surprising if you didn't find something about them to agree with."

"But then I checked out the policies of the Conservatives. And I agree with some of them, too," she admitted.

"That makes sense. A lot of people agree with some of their policies."

"And I've been learning more about the NDP, and they've got a lot of ideas that I agree with. But their organization!" She shook her head.

"Some of their social democratic ideals are put into effect by many Canadian governments, federal or provincial, no matter what party is in power."

"So what does this mean?" she asked.

I sighed. "It means that you're Canadian, my dear. You may find yourself voting Liberal in one election, and Conservative in another. You might become a card-carrying member of a party and vote for them federally, but provincially you might vote for a candidate from a different party. For a city or county election you might choose a candidate with no party affiliation at all."

A big grin spread over her face. "You mean I'm normal?"

"A lot of people feel the way you do, and find some of their own political beliefs in more than one of the major political parties." If that's normal, I must face having a normal daughter. I could cope with that! "Some people vote for a candidate because of who the person is or what he or she will do in the House, no matter what party the candidate belongs to."

"What if there's nobody or no party I want to vote for?"

"There's nearly always somebody you'll want to vote against," I pointed out. "Plus, there's often an Independent running in most ridings in most elections."

"Yeah, sort of a None Of The Above. There ought to be a real None Of The Above, though – a way to show you care enough to vote, even if there's nobody who speaks for you."

"Better to join some party and work to get a candidate you do want to see in office," I suggested. "Or run for office yourself, with or without a party affiliation. There's a whole lot of work that has to get done, outside of elections."

"Now you want me to run for office? But you already want me to go to university, and start a business, and write a book and get the Nobel Peace Prize," my daughter protested. "This time around I'm just going to vote."

Voting isn't always easy. One election, the ballot I opened had five names to choose among. There were two former incumbents, who each had resigned under a cloud. The NDP didn't run in that riding that year. One candidate was hard-working and feminist but represented a party that was neither, and another candidate wanted to bring world peace by levitating his way into the House. The lone Independent had a platform with one plank: no abortions, ever. If there had been a Rhino party candidate in my riding, casting my ballot would have been easy.

Voting takes preparation, whether elections are due in a couple of months or a year. Some people join a political party, or run for office, or hold seminars and peaceful rallies. There's always research to do about the parties and the issues. And mental preparation is definitely needed, even though neither of my teenagers will be running for office yet, and neither would do it like the California candidate who legally changed his name to Sister Boom-Boom and listed his occupation as Nun of the Above. It makes me wonder...

Cat Messages

Never trust a cat to give you your messages.

My cat will not answer the phone. Oh, it may knock the receiver off the hook, or step on the speaker button, but whatever conversation of sniffing and "Hello! We're looking for volunteers!" and meowing that follows will not be recorded.

And when my cat locates the answering machine, it's not to push the button that allows a person at home to record a message just as easily as any caller. Oh, no. In the cat's quest to sleep on top of every warm appliance in the house, the cat will turn round three times, push the button to record a new outgoing message, and settle itself atop the glowing red "Power On" LED.

After that, whenever my answering machine takes a call, the caller doesn't get to hear the brief but witty greeting I recorded. Callers don't even get to hear the machine's default pre-recorded robotic voice saying "After tone, leave message." That robot voice sounds like Stephen Hawking is taking my messages. No, callers are instead treated to the scrabble of claws, the settling of some anonymous bulk, and a vast, distant purring. It's as if a cougar had broken into my farmhouse and was answering my phone.

No wonder the Library Board doesn't leave messages about committee meetings any more.

I'm afraid the only messages that a cat will give are messages which are important to the cat.

"Open the door and let me in! I want to be fed." Luckily, word of mad cow or transgenic grains in pet food hasn't trickled down to my animals, and none of them are picky eaters, unlike humans. People, on the other hand, want to know what's for dinner, and how was it raised and marketed, and how many carbs or trans-fats are in it. Cats have other things on their minds.

"Open the door and let me out! I want the whole Great Outdoors for my litterbox!" This was a bit dicey in winter, until the feline discovery of the space under the deck. Any deck renovations we do this summer will not be any fun.

With all the door-opening, I can understand why some people install cat doors. But the badger that comes by the farm now and then would see a cat door as an invitation, and I don't want to send that sort of message.

At least the cat can't open the door for strangers, but it won't tell me who dropped by while I was out. Do local candidates stop at my farm before an election? I'll never be sure, but I suspect the cat shreds any pamphlets they leave about policies and all-candidates meetings.

I can't even be sure when an election is going to be called. If I leave the newspaper on the coffee table, the cat will sleep on it in the sunbeam from the window. Between sun fading, cat hair and footprints, and some shredding as the cat stretches and sharpens its claws, I can hardly read the newspaper to tell if an election has been called, influence has been peddled, or another country has been invaded to increase our safety. The cat seems smugly unworried about the country or the world or the future, confident that it knows everything it needs to know. Maybe I'll have to try sleeping on the newspaper for a few hours and see if I can learn to absorb information osmotically through my butt like a cat.

One message that I didn't expect a cat to convey is: "Just say no to drugs!" Our cat learned this when it met a relative who is a veterinarian. After a surprise present of neutering, the cat woke up groggy from the anaesthetic to find itself trapped in a carrying cage. It was surrounded by children who stared at the drooling cat with paws jerking and flailing like windmills. That cat walked diagonally for three days after that party.

I'm afraid that the only message a cat can be counted on to deliver is "Time to have a nap." And that, of course, is anytime. Make a lap! Napping with a cat is more relaxing than anything else, at least for a few minutes. Then, back to work, refreshed and calm as a cat.

Silly Season

Well, it's officially the silly season.

Yes, I know it's only May. Silly season started earlier than normal this year. Usually the silly season doesn't start until the weather is too hot to go anywhere without a water bottle and sunblock SPF 50.

Usually I know it's silly season when sports network television runs some game for a tiresome number of hours, played by men I've never met who are each paid more than the entire budget of the Alberta Foundation for the Arts.

Usually silly season is the time when my lamb stew and vegetarian casseroles are turned down by everyone in favour of firing up barbecues full of beefsteak.

Usually silly season is marked by nonsensical announcements by political figures, grandstanding at some public festival run by an over-worked committee with a shoebox full of receipts. There's usually an election somewhere in the country during silly season, even though the result is almost always a foregone conclusion – unless the election is in B.C. And the theme music for silly season is the booming beat of the latest repetitive rap hit single.

But I know that silly season has started early this year, and it's started with a vengeance. For the latest repetitive rap broadcast on the radio was the nonsensical blustering of our premier, appearing at the meeting of a committee he hasn't attended in nine years. Apparently he doesn't like being asked if he has kept expense receipts. It's a pity that the election that will take place before high summer won't be a provincial one; it would be to interesting to learn if Alberta can summon up the attentive and madcap element present in enough B.C. voters to make an effort at keeping politicians accountable.

Good grief! I don't usually spend Mother's Day figuring out who to vote for while putting on industrial-strength sunblock and my long johns. I'd rather buy flowers for my mother, or visit the greenhouses my late mother-in-law used to love.

But, as I said, it is silly season. And it seems to be different this year. Now, my lamb and vegetarian recipes are being requested by everyone. Many people are willing to eat organic hippie food instead of beefsteak bought from the three biggest meat packers in the country, the ones who defied a court order to open their books and account for why cattle sell for so much less than last year but meat doesn't.

And the sports news lately is that the Calgary Flames won some game or other – not the actual Stanley Cup, you understand, but a sufficiently non-seasonal game that crowds actually roamed the streets of Calgary, cheering. For the Flames. I don't even watch any hockey except for minor leagues and the Olympics, and even I know that is truly a sign of Silly Season.

And the weather was hot enough a few days ago that I saw a woman sunbathing in a teeny-weeny bikini on the lawn of her apartment building. The next two days, snow flurries blocked out the sun. Well, this is Alberta. If you don't like the weather, wait five minutes.

All I know is, these days I'm not going anywhere without a water bottle, my sunblock SPF 50 and my winter coat.

Candidates

N ow that the election's been called and the candidates are drumming up support, I'm busy writing when I'm not out in the shed bottle-feeding lambs. Well, at least the lambs give me time to think while my hands are busy. And voting takes a little more thought than juggling bottles for nine hungry lambs. Gotta vote! Can't complain if I don't vote.

So, who's drumming up my support? The party I voted for in the past, the party that has broken and re-formed, the latest party to scatter patronage dollars without getting enough to show for it, the party that is earnest and honest but too small to pay for many ads, and maybe someone standing alone on a soapbox. At least this area doesn't have the situation they do in Athabaska riding, where the mayor of Fort MacMurray is running as a Liberal. Last time around, he ran as a Conservative. I'm not making this up, you know.

This federal election is different from the provincial one that's coming eventually. (It's coming, but I'm not sitting up nights, waiting.) Some important issues are provincial matters, not federal. But there are factors which apply across the country. And they're not impossible to understand.

I got copies of the health care reports written by Roy Romanow and by Don Mazankowski, some months ago. It wasn't as hard to understand them as I expected. Some of the plans make as much sense as changing one's diet and habits, not because of a fad, but because it makes one feel healthy and stronger. So, how have these reports affected your candidates' party platforms?

When you read what these reports have to say, it's worth getting distracted for a moment by what Alberta's Minister of Health has been saying. Apparently Gary Mar feels it's all right to hire his former long-term employee as a consultant – and pay him $200 an hour to produce no reports. Now, I don't have a problem with a few friends or relatives getting real work as consultants or even ambassadors, like Jean Chretien's nephew. The problem with nepotism is when real work doesn't get done, and done at a fair price. I'm sure that hiring friends is one way to feel responsible for their productivity. I'm just not sure that all of our candidates for federal office feel as responsible as the teenager I hired to work in my market garden, who told me his friend was a good worker, too. I'd vote for that teenager, but I wouldn't want to re-elect some people.

I wonder if any of our candidates feel as concerned about safe food products as do the grain farmers debating whether to grow Frankenfood, or as do the customers wondering why genetically-modified soybeans and corn are mixed into most processed food but aren't mentioned on Canadian supermarket labels like they are in Europe. I wonder if anybody is really tracking down whether the lone mad cow was a one-in-a-million mutation or whether this and other illnesses are being caused by agricultural chemicals and spread by bad hygiene. I wonder if enough people care.

But then I hear people discussing the court case of a farmer convicted of growing Round-up Ready canola without paying Monsanto a licensing fee. I hear "bovine spongiform encephalopathy" being pronounced correctly by rednecks and urban artist poseurs. Even with my half-deaf ears, I've heard enough to know that people care. We still wish all our elected officials would do what's right.

So, I hope you'll join me at an all-candidates meeting, or reading the profiles in the paper or listening to CBC radio during supper. After you hear what your local candidates and their parties have planned, ask yourself two questions: what do they say, and what do they do?

Then we'll all go vote, like the people in other countries who line up for hours or days, like the people who dodge bullets or bullies to vote, like the people who defend voters or scrutinize elections, and like the people who work every day to make informed choices possible. Because once we vote, we get to hold our MP accountable.

Bait & Tackle

I 've been asked why so many funny things happen to my family in my stories. Hey, these stories aren't the funny stuff, they're nothing but what I can remember when I eventually find my notebook. And nothing ever happens to us. We have to go looking for it. We can find plenty of nothing in particular just by doing nothing.

Nothing was going on, so me, my brother Karl, his wife Stephanie and our friend Leslie were going to make dinner. There was nothing to eat, so we drove to a grocery store on the way to a friend's house. After buying food, we saw nothing important but a sign in front of another store next to the grocery, a sign which read: "Hunting Fishing Licenses Bait & Tackle."

There really must have been nothing on our minds, because all four of us began thinking furiously after seeing that sign. As we got into the car, Stephanie said brightly: "Hey look, we can get a license to hunt animals by baiting them or tackling them!" She grinned. "I didn't know we needed a license for that – leaping out and tackling animals."

"And there's tackling fish," I said. "I took a class at the community centre the other day, learning how to tackle fish. A fishing tackle is different from a football tackle, eh?" I nudged Leslie as we all did up our seatbelts.

"Yeah? How do they do it?" Leslie asked, as Karl started the car. I could see her thinking hard, to keep the conversation going. "With a tackle box?"

"There's one!" Stephanie crowed. "Leap! Sploosh!"

"And some people just do it for recreation, they don't want to eat the fish," Karl put in. He spoke a little more slowly, as he was turning the car out of the parking lot into traffic. "So, like Touch Football, they just play Touch Fishing and they lean out of the boat and just touch the fish. Scare the wits out of it, too." He turned onto Otter Point Road. "Uhh-oooh what the heck was that?"he asked, in a fishy kind of voice. "Boy, was that weird! You'll never believe what just happened to me, Charlie, something pink just came out of nowhere and touched me. Ooooough. Dunno what it was, but it tasted like beer."

"We could always get a bait license," I said after a while. "So, like, how do you bait a bear?" Nothing came to mind at first.

"Put out lots of food in the same place every day," said Karl shortly, as the road veered around a golf course and he narrowly avoided golfers driving home from the nineteenth hole. He has answers for everything. Nothing gets past him.

Leslie nodded. "So they get used to coming by."

"Then you hide up a tree," I suggested, "and say things to bug them like 'Ya mudda wears army boots!'"

Leslie stuck her tongue out at an imaginary bear, far below her imaginary perch in a tree. "You smell like an old coat!"

In a deep, rolling and completely fake British accent, Stephanie intoned, "Ya mudder wears army boots and ya fadda smelt of elderberries." She knows all the most obscure Monty Python quotes.

"Revile him for taking handouts," I suggested. "National Parks Layabout! Yah! You'd never make it in a Real Forest without an Affirmative Action Program!"

"I think tackling bears would be harder," Leslie said thoughtfully. "Especially after baiting them."

"That would only be by accident, if you fell out of the tree," Stephanie pointed out.

"Better get both kinds of license," Karl told us as he parked the car. "Just in case."

Nothing much to this story. But we had fun, even though nothing was happening. And clearly, there was nothing more to say.

Vote

It may not be winter according to the calendar, but we've sure changed seasons. When my dad was a kid up in the Coal Branch, they had two seasons: winter and "bad sledding," also known as "bug season." Well, there's finally no mosquitoes around. But snow or no snow, the sledding isn't good enough yet to be winter, not by local standards, anyway. And at least this season, we can look forward to two elections; not just the expected municipal election but a provincial one that's sorely needed.

So! Before deciding how to vote, it's time to ask some questions.

When you pick up the phone to call your local constituency offices to get the skinny on the party platforms for your local candidates, pick up your phone bill, too. Look how much more you're paying for basic telephone service since privatization. Are you getting more service, or better? Are the bills staying steady, or matching inflation, or climbing? Maybe this will give you some questions to ask your candidates about their parties' plans for The Utilities Formerly Known as Public.

When you turn on a light one evening, to write a letter to your local candidate, take a quick look at your electricity bill, too. There's a little graph to tell you how much power you're using these days compared to what you used last year. Are you using more power, or less, even during the winter cold snaps? Are there brownouts in your area? And how long did repairs take the last time your area had a downed power line or transformer?

I'm not wondering whether my power bill will go up – the power companies already announced increases, just to handle the increased volume of calls. Apparently a great number of people are inquiring about their bills. I know I'd like to inquire what each party's candidate thinks about the dubious merits of privatizing a public utility to the extent that a profit is skimmed off by those who generate the electricity, those who distribute it, those who deliver it and those who maintain the grid. Oh, and those who answer the phones and now those who send the bills.

If you can do all that math and reading and writing, thank a teacher. It's still possible to get a basic education in this province, but it's hard to get a good job without a post-secondary education. These days, going to university or college or a technical institute isn't the affordable effort it was years ago when I was a student. Tuition fees have climbed at several times the rate of inflation. And student loans mean punishing debt loads. So how do your candidates feel about tuition fee increases?

There are universities in the Western world which do NOT pay so much of their operating costs through tuition fees – heck, there are some that don't charge citizens any tuition fees at all! But you won't find any of those in Alberta. Now, that would be a nice thing to do with some of those oil revenues: free tuition for citizens at accredited colleges and universities.

About those oil revenues: the Parkland Institute's website points out some interesting statistics. Alberta collects $4 for each barrel of crude oil. Sounds like a lot? Not when compared to the $11 per barrel collected by Iceland. Is there a party that can explain this to me?

Now, some candidates are independents without party affiliations. It'll take a little research to determine whether any one independent is a free-thinking maverick who works alone, or someone who just doesn't work well with others.

These are just some of the questions to ask when deciding how to vote: starting points for dialogues with your candidate, with your friends or with yourself. Funny how there's a lot to think about without even mentioning health care or the provincial debt or conflicts of interest, let alone genetically modified food organisms or mad cow. But at least in this country we can ask questions – smart or dumb, vague or pointed – without fear. And we can vote. And we can write to our MLAs and cabinet ministers, and sometimes even get an answer back.

Letters

A couple of times, I've suggested in this column that people write to their Members of Parliament or Members of the Legislature. It's not hard – letters to the Ottawa offices of MPs don't even have to have postage! Lots of people write to their MPs and MLAs. But I get letters back. And not just a form letter reply.

It started when I wrote to Alberta's Health Minister, Gary Mar. My husband has sleep apnea, and a specialist referred him to the Sleep Disorders Lab, to book a test. The waiting list was 90 weeks long. The staff at the Sleep Disorders Lab were so helpful to us that I asked them how I could help them. "Well, you could write to the Health Minister," they suggested.

You bet I wrote to the Health Minister: a letter every week, with a copy sent to my local MLA, Dave Broda. I explained how sleep apnea makes my husband stop breathing when he falls asleep. I explained how my husband had waited months already to see a specialist. The doctor had prescribed this test to measure how many times a night my husband stopped breathing, and how much it was affecting his blood oxygen, his heart and his brain. I explained about the increased risk of heart conditions or strokes, or even car crashes and other accidents, for people with untreated sleep apnea.

I wrote every week.

It took three letters before I got a reply: a "thank-you-for-your-concern" form letter. That did not stop me. My next letters began with: "Thank you for your letter ..." and informed the Health Minister of how my husband still stopped breathing several times a night. I described how the Sleep Disorders Lab in Edmonton had four beds at that time for all the referrals from Northern Alberta. In six months an expansion was planned – to eight beds. They had a long enough waiting list that twelve beds could easily be filled every night, if they had enough funding.

I got a second reply from the Health Minister's office: a suggestion that my husband and I talk to his doctor about moving his name up the waiting list.

I thanked Gary Mar for his reply, but informed him that the specialist had already assessed my husband's condition. I was not writing to the Minister to appeal to have my partner tested ahead of all the other people who were waiting their turn, who had been assessed by doctors as having a more immediate need. I was writing because a waiting list of 90 weeks was intolerable, when the technology and training existed to give patients a test, to see what treatment was necessary.

I wrote every week, over that Christmas season, wishing the Health Minister and my local MLA season's greetings. I asked them if they enjoyed holiday food, visiting with friends and enjoying a cup of cheer, and explained that my husband was eating and drinking moderately and keeping regular hours. This is how a person with sleep apnea can help his or her condition, but it is no substitute for the test and treatment.

Eventually I got a third letter from the Health Minister's office, with the suggestion that my husband could consider going to a private clinic for testing.

I replied to Gary Mar that in addition to two part-time jobs, I was working as an artist's model in order to earn the money a private clinic would charge. Yes, I was taking off my clothes in front of strangers to earn the money to pay for my husband's health care. And I hoped he would think of that every time he recommends that someone go to a private clinic.

I found it abominable that the Minister of Health would recommend a private clinic instead of adequately funding public health care. Private clinics are appropriate for cosmetic surgery and other voluntary treatments. But profiteering off the suffering of desperate people is not acceptable.

I then added that my husband had actually had his test. Someone else had died, waiting for his or her own turn, and my husband was the first one the Sleep Disorders Lab could reach on their list of patients who can scramble to fill vacancies.

In this election, I take a particular pride in NOT voting for the party in power. I will not vote for the local representative of the Cabinet with the Health Minister who told my husband to go to a private clinic when he stopped breathing in his sleep.

Hope

It's the holiday season again, and I'm summoning up my holiday spirit. Bring out the canned milk of human kindness! Let's have some peace on Earth, and goodwill to all mankind – at least until New Year's Eve.

I'm not sure whether this Christmas will be a quiet time of looking back over a year of international fears and hopes, or a celebration of a coming year of peace. But if even Israel has enough optimists to form another coalition government, well, I should find my inner optimist, too. First, I'll try a little looking back.

So, I'm at my parents' house this holiday season, looking through old photographs and talking with my brother. "Ever look at your old class photos?" he said. "Grade Six. Everybody looked at their own faces in the group and thought – Oh, no! I look like a dork! Everybody must be looking at my picture and thinking that I'm a dork!"

He is so right. I remembered being in that Grade Six group photo and thinking, I've ruined the picture. Everyone will look at their class photos for years and think that I'm a dork!

"But look at the other faces," said my brother. "Everybody is a dork. It's just part of being eleven. And of trying to get so many kids in one picture at the same time." Each of us kids was afraid the others would think of us forever as the only dork, if not in Grade Six then in softball practice or Scouts. But each kid in my class photos had weird hair, or crooked glasses, or an itch, or was looking out the window, or smiling at some inner thought. And as for our clothes – did we really think bell-bottoms went with golf shirts? Everybody's inner optimist was showing, and their inner dork, too.

"A lot of people go around afraid all the time of looking like a dork," My brother said. "We should just get over it. Everybody looks like a dork sometime. But even if people notice, they're not thinking about us forever. Later, they're thinking about sometime when they looked like a dork themselves."

And you know, even if there really is someone somewhere who really does think of me as a complete dork, well, that person wouldn't be much fun to hang around with anyway.

I'm going to try to accept our dork nature as part of our humanity, not worth crying over for long. And it wouldn't hurt to pay more attention to our optimism, and exercise that part of ourselves

This Christmas I take what hope I can – and it is a deep, sustaining kind of hope, not the faint and wistful kind – from the news that this year's Nobel Peace Prize has gone to an African woman who has been planting trees for years. At first glance, planting a tree might not look much like working for peace. But she's built her community, developed sustainable businesses, recovered farmland and improved watersheds and weather, and been active in government, all through decades of planting trees with her neighbours. She didn't cancel her tree-planting appointment one afternoon just to hold an impromptu press conference about winning the Nobel Peace Prize. She is a woman who keeps her promises – and schedules the press conference for the next day.

On the news, I watched as she accepted the prize with grace and dignity, with her big work-hardened hands on the podium and her tall, dark figure wrapped in bright orange clothing from her own region of Africa. In the news photos, she didn't look anything like the dignitaries who gathered to honour her award, except for their bright eyes full of hope.

This year, we can make hope happen, with whatever capacity we each have for hope. We just had an election, but voting isn't the only thing we can do to be active in our communities and to put hope in our lives. Plant a tree. Support someone's education or small business. Teach a kid how to fly a kite. Because we can have or make at least some peace on Earth.

Winter

I'm going to have to face it – the real winter's here. Real winter starts after Christmas, when you're happy after all to have found a fine set of booster cables or long johns under the tree. And winter's not going away for quite a while. I know it's really winter because not only are New Canadian immigrants wearing hooded parkas, tuques, mitts and scarves, while toughened Prairie dwellers wear hooded parkas and maybe gloves. I know it because I saw teenagers waiting at the bus stop, and they'd done up their coats.

So far this winter, I've had the opportunity to see a lot of people while riding public transit buses in the Edmonton area, as well as Ottawa, Toronto, Mississauga, Vancouver and Victoria. All ages of people ride the bus sometimes, and all income levels – even luxury cars will break down sometime and leave rich drivers stranded. I've seen a woman in a fur coat stand in line on Granville Street to board a bus behind a scruffy guy, and the breeze brought me the mingled scents of her perfume and his woolen coat.

When one isn't driving through traffic, there's plenty of time to notice faces of the people all around, on buses and sidewalks, in businesses and libraries, at home or in the parks. I've seen a lot of faces from other places during the last two months: shivering blue faces of immigrants, chattering kids on the way to home or school, workers and retired folk. And I've had the leisure time to compare these faces with those I see around the big and little towns of Sturgeon County.

You know what? You people look grumpy!

Oh, it's not that you never smile. It's that the smiles look so different from the usual expressions on your faces.

Is everyone on the way to a parent-teacher conference at the junior high school? Are all of you waiting until payday to get a broken filling replaced? Did everyone look out the front door a moment ago and see missionaries coming up the stairs?

Honestly, most people around here are sour-faced much of the time. Maybe drivers are concentrating on the radio news while they drive – goodness knows, news reports can make anyone feel sad or angry. Maybe those tough guys are being resolute and strong while standing in line – it beats shouting at a busy clerk. Maybe those ladies are looking through their purses for prescription medicine but their safety-top pill bottles have rolled to the bottom.

But I don't think so. I don't think that three-quarters of the people in Sturgeon County believe that polite public behaviour means schooling one's face to a grim demeanour. I think they don't know better. I think they don't know they look like the villagers who lived down the hill from Victor Frankenstein's laboratory, who were never too busy to pick up some torches and pitchforks and go after his monster.

So I'm telling you all: Lighten up!

You're living in one of the best countries in the world. Even if you don't like something, you can fix it or try to fix it, or just complain about it without being shot.

Yes, it's winter, and may be winter here till May. But if you don't have a warm coat, get on over to any of several charities and your neighbours will give you one.

Yes, you may have bad news. If not now, sooner or later something makes each of us sad or angry. Welcome to the club. And give your friends a chance to know from your face whether this is the day you got bad news or just the day your shoelace broke.

Yes, you may be busy adults with responsibilities. But you don't look like brave heroes. You look like football coaches who just smelled something bad.

I've had about enough of people who scowl instead of wearing a hat with a brim to shade their eyes, or people who squint instead of putting on their eyeglasses. It distorts your face, and so distorts your own mood and the moods of all who see you, even out of the corners of their eyes as they pass.

There are too many of us who forget to start the day with an awareness of our health and strength. There are some of us who forget to go to work with pride in each step of our labour. And there are far too many of us who forget that the most renewable resource of all is the resolution to do good, and to take joy in the good that comes to us.

So, crack a smile from time to time, eh? Maybe smile at someone else, or when you're alone. Every person who gets off a bus in Victoria thanks the driver; do you do that? Put on your red shoes and dance the blues, once in a while.

I'm going to face it myself, and try to remember to smile when the phoebes are chirping in the bare trees this winter, even though my bum ears now hear only "chirp" instead of their distinctive "fee-bee" tones. My hands and feet will still be cold, but maybe my face will be a little warmer.

Wealth

I've been going through neighbourhoods where all the houses look shut up, tight as an airlock. This goes beyond the fact that it's winter and we all want to keep our warm air inside the house instead of heating the Great Outdoors, as my dad says. It's not just that all the windows are closed, and all the doors are shut in some neighbourhoods, but the windows are covered with blinds and don't look out into the yard or street anyway. And the doors have no windows in 'em, and aren't really made to stand open, even in good weather. There's something more inviting about a house with a screen door, the wooden door propped open inside it and yes, a latch locking the screen door against casual burglary.

Most of these houses without screen doors or kitchen windows someone can look through and wave, most are new and expensive. But are they signs of wealth or of luxury? Wealth sustains us – it shelters us and supplies our needs, with confidence. Wealth may sustain, but luxury corrupts.

I was thinking of the wealth that our country's abundance brings to us. We have an abundance of resources, of opportunities for work in production and distribution and cultural matters, and an abundance of people ready to do and make and enjoy all these opportunities – people who generally have the ability and education to make the best of our lot.

Wealth as a work is linked to weal and health and wield. It is a strong and active thing, stronger by doing than by lying in reserve. Where riches may tempt us to idleness, we can find wealth instead in our exercise of our abilities.

It is not dollars that feed us. It is food that fills a belly. And where there is grain and meat and greens, it is a crime when any go hungry for want of mere dollars and work. Wealth that feeds and shelters people is true wealth, and the work that sustains people is noble.

Wealth brings us confidence. Confidence that a meal is coming, and it is good. Confidence in our shelter for rest and sleep. Confidence that other people are our neighbours, not our enemies. Confidence in our health and in the worthiness of our labour, whatever it may be. Confidence in our future.

I've been impressed anew by the wealth of our schools – an expression of our confidence in our future. There is luxury, yes, in multiple computers and in pop machines and mP3 players, but there is also the wealth shown in what may appear at first to be plainly furnished rooms decorated with colourful bits of paper.

I look at the strength and solidness of buildings, constructed with union labour, intended to last decades in challenging climates. I look at floors and walls that can be kept hygienic and clean, of windows and plenty of electric light. I see desks and books – not just a few, but a serious effort to have a place and a book for every child, not just the lucky or the wealthy. The teachers work with confidence that their skills and knowledge are worth sharing, that they are part of a professional association for teaching and standards, and that they may work unharrassed by arbitrary political turmoil.

For weeks the news has carried stories of the devastation of the tsunami and its aftermath. But the wretched poverty endured by some survivors is not due only to the natural disaster. Natural disasters can happen anywhere – and do. But poverty isn't what happens when your house is destroyed (thatched hut or brick bungalow). Poverty is what happens when there is no doctor or nurse for your injuries, and no help from others to make your new home, so that you may also help others to make theirs. Poverty is what happens when the resources do exist to heal and feed and shelter you, but those resources are diverted or withheld by self-serving opportunist. Any political, military or personal agenda that diverts or withholds necessary resources from people in need is at the very least suspect, and usually bogus.

It's worth remembering that the number of people who died on the day the earthquake and tsunami struck is matched every day in Africa. And those people die, not just from drought or other natural disaster, but from human actions or the lack of needed human actions. It's also worth remembering that our own wealth here can be measured not only in our fine homes, and in the confidence we have in our continued work and health and shelter, but in our compassion for others who need the help of neighbours – the help we each have had. So, I don't mind if your house doesn't have a screen door – so long as there's a metaphorical screen door on your mind, instead of an airlock.

Perspective

I'm trying to keep perspective on the things I do. Usually any one day's activities won't save my life, but that's no excuse for not riding my bike. The exercise does me good.

When I'm in town, I've been enjoying riding a second-hand bike I picked up for a song. It's not actually a bike – it's got three wheels, which makes it a tricycle. All right, go ahead. Make your jokes. I don't mind. I fell off my old bicycle too many times, because my wonky ears have no sense of balance. Now, with the large basket between the two rear wheels, I can get groceries or haul my library books around. I've gained stability at low speeds by giving up hope of reaching high speeds. It's given me perspective.

On bike trails, I see a lot of walkers and bikers, and most smile to see my three-wheeler go by. Yes, I get passed all the time, by serious bikers and their little kids all zooming along in a pack. I also get passed by joggers.

That part gets me down, but I try to cope. I share stories of my little exercise rides, training for health, with my friends, and they tell me their stories. One friend is a volunteer firefighter in Nelson, who sent me pictures of herself and her team training for river rescues. And she told me a story that gives me perspective.

Did you hear about the woman whose life was saved by chocolate?

I'm not making this up, you know.

She's an X-ray technician, heading to work at a hospital near Nelson, BC at about 1:00 in the morning in February. Her little truck skidded off the highway, and rolled down an embankment. It came to a halt upside-down in the middle of a river.

73

The driver was okay. But when she'd wrestled her way out of her seatbelt and the airbag, she couldn't open the doors or windows and the vehicle was filling with cold water. The back window had broken, but a small table in back was blocking that way out. She found an air bubble near the floor of her vehicle, and the water stopped rising when it got to her chin. There were chunks of river ice floating around. When she ducked under to find her purse, she got her cell phone but it was soaked and wouldn't work.

In the pitch dark, with ice water up to her chin, she knew she was going to die. At least she would see her late husband in heaven, she thought. But she couldn't stand the thought of leaving her children orphaned. And her new fiance was a widower himself – her death would be the second loss for him. She had to live.

Then she found a plastic box of chocolates floating with her. She'd bought it herself to give her family. She'd been on a diet for a year, and hadn't eaten any chocolate.

But when those Ferrero Rochers bumped into her, there was no doubt in her mind. Screw the diet! She ate chocolate, and bicycled her legs in the cold water to keep warm, and tried to believe that her fiance would come looking for her.

And of course, he did.

The hospital called him to say she hadn't arrived, so he went looking for her. There was nothing visible from the highway, but he went back and forth, got out and stumbled down to the river in the dark, where he eventually spotted the wheels of her vehicle in the middle of the icy river. When he screamed, to his surprise she answered.

She'd been in the water for an hour by then, and it took another hour for the Beasley VFD to rescue her. All the vehicle doors were jammed, and they had to winch it carefully to pry a door open without losing her air bubble. Two trained rescuers in dry suits hauled her out and she was hustled to hospital. Her body temperature was so low, the doctors don't know how she survived. But they suspect that eating a box of chocolates gave her energy to replace the heat she lost to the icy river.

And the next day, she embraced her rescuers, who simply had to see and speak with her. For years they had trained in river rescues, and worn dry suits to retrieve people who had died in similar accidents. But to save a survivor – well, that put all the training exercises and all the sad retrievals in perspective.

Perspective can help us see how each small effort can help us reach an extraordinary goal. It can help us understand what action is required, and when patience and persistance is a virtue. And when it helped that woman realize that diets have to fit into your real life experience, it saved her life.

I don't have that kind of perspective yet. But I'm making Christmas cards for my friend to use, with a picture of her on a VFD training exercise. And I'm trying to keep riding my bike, even as joggers pass me – on the flat – one step at a time.

Amber

"I never touch anyone else's crystals," my cousin declared. Jet beads hung around her neck and glittered at her ears. "Some people think it's important to keep them charged with your own energy, so I look but don't touch. Not unless I'm invited." Then she smiled, and added: "Will you tell me about your amber necklace?"

It's charged enough for any New Ager, charged with such a happy memory that I didn't mind at all if she handled it. My cousin's love for semi-precious stones is so obvious that it was a pleasure to see my amber beads in her hands.

I bought the necklace in Winnipeg, a few years ago. Winnipeg may not seem like an exotic vacation destination, except to someone from Flin Flon, but I was visiting there during the World Science Fiction Convention. There's no amber to be found anywhere near Winnipeg, except what's brought in by dealers and stores. I got this from a dealer during the 52nd annual WorldCon.

A WorldCon actually is an exotic vacation destination, even the one time it was held in Winnipeg. Quite apart from the charms of the host city itself, a WorldCon is a vacation from mundane concerns. It's a five-day holiday to indulge in whatever interests you most about science fiction, from books, films and tv to costumes, games and emerging discoveries in real science. It's exotic enough for anyone's taste. I shared an elevator with people of four racial heritages – one dressed as a Klingon, another draped in costume jewels and veils, a best-selling author and a tweed-jacketed academic who'd just been awarded tenure.

And in every crowd in every meeting room in that convention centre, I kept seeing one or two people here and there wearing necklaces of amber beads. Some of the necklaces were strings of smooth, polished ovals, but most were rough, uneven shapes, only lightly polished. The beads seemed almost to glow, even in indoor light.

I tracked down the source finally. In the Dealer's Room – a meeting hall crowded with tables – I wandered past phaser guns and autographed books and handmade chain mail to a table full of jewellry. On a stand hung dozens of amber necklaces, rope after rope of beads, in all the natural shades of amber from almost clear to dark brown. In a glass case were amber pendants on fine chains of gold or silver. Some of the pendants had inclusions – seeds, pine needles, or insects – trapped thousands of years ago when the sap had oozed from pine trees and slowly hardened into amber.

"Where did you get so much amber?" I asked the dealer. He paused in opening yet another package of little boxes.

"The best pieces I got wholesale," he explained. "I finished polishing them and setting them in their findings, on rings or chains. But the beads, well, I got most of those in Poland."

He told me he was walking on a beach, looking out over the Baltic sea, walking along a shoreline where small chunks of amber wash up in the waves now and then. After a while he noticed someone was walking toward him, toward the west, walking along the shore from the direction of the little countries that were formerly part of the Soviet Union. Eventually he met the stranger on the beach. There was plenty of room to pass, but the stranger came up to him, and asked: "You want to buy some amber?" He opened his coat. Inside the long coat, the man was hung with rope after rope of beads – chunks of amber strung into necklaces.

These were the necklaces the dealer brought back for sale, here at the WorldCon. The prices he had set on them varied according to size and quality, but the simplest necklaces were only $14 Can. That just happened to be what I had budgeted for food for the next day.

There wasn't any real decision to make at that point, except which shade of amber I wanted. I chose a bright golden colour, like the liquid honey that bees make from fireweed blossoms.

Amber usually costs much more than I paid, but I believe this dealer was considering the simple necklaces in the same way a major grocery store considers a sale on strawberries. Even after advertising a loss leader price on strawberries, the store makes its profits on whipping cream and shortcake and the rest of a customer's grocery order.

I missed three meals to pay for that necklace, without complaint. Yes, it was simpler and less fine than the one my friend bought, or the grand one I saw around the neck of a best-selling author. But each of us fasted a day in order to buy our necklaces. And as for the other people wearing amber – I talked to a dozen among the hundred I saw in that crowd of five thousand – a little conversation in elevators revealed that they had done the same.

That's the energy that's in this necklace, for me, I told my cousin. The finding of something fine in a display of goods from all over, the feeling of a sense of community, the choice to indulge myself in a lasting treat instead of yet another meal. It's not a gem to hide in a safety deposit box – it's something to wear and enjoy in my real life.

Optimism

Optimism. They say spring is a time for optimism. I'm finding optimism where I can. Sometimes I don't have to look very hard for it. Hope comes easy when I look at a new book contract or my daughter's photography assignments. Also, we've just come through an entire season free of most of the hullabaloo of NHL hockey. If that doesn't make you feel like an optimist, you haven't been playing oldtimers' hockey at the arena, or coaching kids' sports, or training for the 10 K run.

As for all the young up-and-coming hockey players who missed out on their NHL dreams this year – solidarity, brothers. Been there. Ever wondered what happened to Canadian writers and editors that year the biggest book distributor in the country went bust because the biggest bookstore chain didn't pay its bills? It was a year of drought, too, on the farm. But this spring I'm writing a new book, and I've finally found a source for peas with purple pods. And in the 10 K run I walked amid all the runners and wheelchairs, finishing in 108 minutes, 59 seconds. The frontrunners could have run the race three times around by then, of course, but it was a grand day to enjoy a walk.

Who wouldn't be full of hope, with the queen herself coming to town?

It's a cliché that Spring is a time for optimism. But we get clichés from experience, and particularly from experiences we remember. And it's in spring that I remember the order of things beginning.

The order in which ornamental trees bloom – cherry, plum, magnolia, hawthorn and dogwood. The fruit trees, too – pear, apple, cherry and plum, later and simpler than their showy cousins but with the promise of harvest to come, tart and sweet.

The lambs and calves born in lingering cold weather are grown enough to eat the first new grass.

The fields are turned, to open them for seed. And above the black earth, the warmed updraft of air lifts the flocks of geese that have learned to let it raise them into the high winds. The migrating flocks follow their same routes each year, and they've been riding that updraft from our fields since our farm first went under the plow, ninety-nine years ago.

It takes optimism to fly north into the lands where winter clings, and chase Spring into the cold water and ground. It's the best kind of optimism, too, the kind that involves hard work and health and healing. Anyone can hope, and cross their fingers. Mere hope is an easy virtue. But it takes a real optimist to plant potatoes in a spring like we had four years ago, when the trees on our farm didn't open their leaves until the first week of June.

And it takes an optimist to take the winter months (which are never idle, even for farmers) for training in music, or commercial baking, or visual arts. These things may bring us new work and new income. And even without that hope, these things feed us and sustain us as we do them. Who put the colour in your working shirt, so it's not just the colour of dirt? Who made the songs you sing when you're busy, or on a long drive? Sometimes a song is just a babble of abcs for a child learning not to be grumpy when it's tired. Sometimes a song is sung again for years, like hymns in the church where my father-in-law was married at seventy-three this spring.

Optimists, the pair of them, bride and groom. I am only an amateur, proud of their hope and their marriage and the astounding changes they are making in their lives. Their families' good wishes for their health and happiness together are matched by a string of people across the country. We can't all be there when called on short notice, but that could never stop our thoughts being with them. And our hopes.

Proud

I've been thinking about all the things to be proud of in our Armed Forces.

What's on my mind is not just the heroes. I've met peacekeepers who have put their bodies in the path of danger, who have been a living example of our belief that there are alternatives to fighting and war. I've met Canadian astronauts, who have flown on the space shuttles and trained with the crews who died when first Challenger, and then Columbia came to a fiery end. But I'm trying to think today of the ordinary people and their equipment, put to good use where they are needed.

During the Great Flood in Southern Manitoba, our Armed Forces were there when needed – and some of these experienced servicemen were later sent as advisors to deal with the recent flooding in Europe. During the Great Ice Storm back east, our Armed Forces were essential, as they proved to be in Victoria's Great Blizzard of '98, where four feet of snow fell one January night.

But I don't have pictures of these soldiers in action. I do have photographs, however, of my daughter's boyfriend at a military base, being trained in the use of explosives. The photos show a sequence: James holding up equipment, James and an instructor working on the equipment, James huddled behind a bunker, and then James standing proudly in the hole he had just blasted. From what I hear, explosives are also used to trigger avalanches safely, and to clear mountain passes. But rather than dwell on that in a season when two avalanches near Revelstoke have just killed fourteen hikers and skiers, I linger over the last photo: James with his squad. All dirty, all tired, all happy. Four young men and a young woman of various races, all wearing the same drab fatigues. Go team! That's the face of the Canadian Armed Forces in my memory.

The Armed Forces are a part of ordinary life, for my family, from my huband's time in the Reserves, my father's time in the Navy, and the military base near our farm, There was an Air Show at Namao Base about ten years ago, with local planes and military aircraft and a visiting fighter jet from Ukraine. My family went through the base with the crowds. We got to walk through a Canadian Hercules aircraft, one of those that cruise over our farm, and an even bigger C5 aircraft from the USA. Best of all was the chance to meet a Search and Rescue technician and see all his gear.

This man looked like an astronaut in his protective suit. He would routinely parachute out of a Hercules, wearing a pack the size of a refrigerator. Anyone in any kind of trouble – say, a plane crash up North – would be able to look up at an approaching SARTech and know that here was help, food, shelter, and a radio in the hands of a paramedic with a medical kit.

Later I went with my kids onto the runway and got to go into the cockpit of an American B52 bomber. The pilot explained to us how fast the jet could travel, and how many pounds of bombs it could carry. "That's way faster than the Hercules we toured today," I said. "We see them flying over our farm. The Hercules has that back door, and can drop crates of supplies on parachutes, without even having to land." The pilot agreed that it was a versatile aircraft on aid missions overseas, and pointed out that the American C5 was big enough to carry large vehicles driven up either its front or rear ramps. We even chatted about the Mars water bombers, war planes now used by forest-firefighting crews on Vancouver Island.

Then I asked what else can the B52 do – high speed surveillance? Transport essential personnel? "Nothing, really," said the pilot. "Just the bombs." The pilot had the grace to blush and look away over the airfield, where cropdusters were parked next to cargo planes and troop transports.

As my family walked away, the visiting jet fighter from Ukraine was racing overhead, demonstrating a military manoeuvre they called the "kohl-i-kohl"—a steep climb to stall, and fall, and climb again to stall and fall.

Sports

We can tell a lot about a person from what we can see. Or at least, we think we can. That driver of a sedan with a mountain bike strapped on back? Just ride it, man. An SUV with a kayak strapped on top, next to a coffee shop? All the coffee you can buy won't float that boat till you go to the beach!

I'm used to the bikers passing me cheerfully at high speed on the bike paths, and once in a long while one makes a wisecrack about my wobbling progress. Loss of balance and some hearing doesn't show like a blind person's white cane. I swear that I'm going to have to start carrying an ordinary cane when I go for a walk, just as a visual signal to others that I may wobble. What signal would do the same on my bike, I'm not sure. You'd think a three-wheeler with a reflective triangle on the back would be pretty obvious. This is no high performance vehicle. It has two speeds: slow, and stop.

I'm also used to the reaction when I take my bike helmet off, and my mop of silver hair is exposed. Store clerks, with courtesy and friendliness, offer me the senior's discount. I'm forty-four. Yes, I have the hands of a market gardener, and the finely-honed body of a freelance writer. So, maybe these clerks and the people who give me their bus seats are just seeing an opportunity to be nice. As for dying my hair, well, my two fashion advisers forbid it. My grown kids tell me that my silver hair looks beautiful. If you can't believe a professional photographer and a man with six earrings and a home-made shirt, whose advice are you going to take?

Now, this summer I'm out of the market garden and have enough time to be looking for a leisure activity to burn off some energy. I tried kayaking, for the first time in twenty-five years. Oh, I've been canoeing dozens of times in the interval. But a canoe is a two-person boat, really, and it's hard to handle on your own. As for how it is to handle with a partner who believes that his big, strong shoulders mean he should be the stern paddler on his second time in a canoe, well, I leave that to the imagination. Kayaks are different.

We tried a bunch of different kayaks, one afternoon at a lake. A local boating store offers free try-outs, knowing full well that if the first time is free, there's definitely going to be a second time and some purchases and so on. We tried stubby little river kayaks and long, slim sea kayaks and versatile mid-size ones. We drooled over the ones with go-faster stripes on their fibreglass sides. And we didn't even try the two-seater kayaks at all. In a boating emergency, of course, my partner and I would simply use a two-seater kayak to save our lives and so on. But in the interests of not having a boating emergency, we looked at single-person boats.

And we learned some things. Big, strong shoulders mean a person's centre of gravity is way higher, and tipping is more likely. Also, having no sense of balance is less of an issue when my centre of gravity is so low. And best of all, upper body strength means less than knowing how to do a J-stroke with a two-bladed paddle. It was a nice realization, after all the bike rides where my partner cheerfully rides circles around me or quietly grinds his teeth as he patiently follows behind my snail's pace. I could paddle faster, straighter and farther than my fella, and without any pulled muscles afterward.

My sheaf of gray hair isn't a factor when a sun hat is crammed over it. I'm plenty strong enough to lift one end of a long sea kayak or carry a river kayak all by myself. And there are plenty of places to take one: lakes, streams, and out by my parents' house there's a quiet ocean bay.

Is it any surprise that we bought a cheap second-hand kayak? A short but versatile one, made of tough plastic so we can use it without fuss. When my partner realized that this one had a cup holder, our choice was made. "Kayaking with my coffee cup," he said. "Does life get any better?" This little boat darts along like the swallows that dipped and spun past on the first day we paddled it around a lake.

So, now we've joined the ranks of those with a kayak strapped to the roof of their car. Yes, it spends most of the time tucked under the deck. But six times in three weeks, he's lifted it onto the roof of our sedan, and strapped his mountain bike to the back. If we're going somewhere, he might as well ride his bike while waiting for a turn with the kayak. Can you tell by looking at our car next to the coffee shop, that we're on our way to have fun?

Fear and Horror

When bombs explode, they blow apart more than chemicals and containers, more than buildings or vehicles. More is blown apart than even the bodies of the people hurt or killed by a blast. Barriers in the minds of people are taken down: barriers against fear and horror, barriers in the minds of survivors and people nearby. Sometimes people who never imagined that they would ever be subject to this kind of fear and horror begin to realize that there is no effective barrier in the world against all dangers of this kind.

Just days before the recent bombs in London, I attended a science fiction conference. The panel discussions at such conferences naturally touch on books and films, whether works of fine literature or popular trivia, and the interaction of fantasy or horror with science and the world at large. One editor spoke of her surprise that when she edited a book on the architecture of horror, there were some readers eager to use her book as a kind of reference book for home renovations. They were using it to bring the elements of horror movies and frightening stories into their home lives. Frankly, it creeped her right out.

Her husband spoke up then, from the audience, to tell of the greatest moment of horror in his own life. He's an editor as well, for a major publisher in New York City, and was commuting into that city on when he heard a radio report of the first airliner striking the World Trade Center. He went on to his dentist appointment, where he heard radio reports of the second plane striking the second tower. And then the third plane fell.

It certainly sounded like a horrific moment: laying back with sharp things grinding away at one's teeth, while airplanes are falling out of the sky. But the horror for him was realizing that such violence, visible from his office window, was even possible. He had thought that it would never happen "here" – only far away. And he had come to understand that this experience was changing his tastes in fiction and film, and affecting his work and the selection of books he made for publication.

It's not like he was uneducated or ignorant. But the man is nearly sixty years old and it took September 11th for him to realize he lived in a glass house. And I wasn't about to let him shanghai the panel discussion onto his own agenda.

"We're not going to get into a contest of "The Most Horror In My Own Life," I told him. "Because A-1, I trump you. But mostly because, we're here to discuss how to write about horror." And I told him and the audience about how Stewart Brand had written of an earthquake in San Francisco, and how to find the article in Whole Earth Review and on the internet. Brand wrote of his thoughts when his bookshelf fell on his head, realizing that he was a moron for hanging a shelf over his desk in an earthquake zone. He wrote of checking his building and then going out into his neighbourhood to be a strong, helpful person. Brand admitted that he'd walked right past his car with his hiking boots, tough pants and folding shovel in the trunk and messed about in his sneakers and light chinos when helping people out of collapsed houses. And how he couldn't pull out one trapped couple as their house caught fire. As the injured husband managed to scrape free, he was still unable to free his wife from the wreckage. Brand heard what they said to each other, heard her tell him to try to escape, heard her forgive him. And he did not write their last conversation in his article.

"But I'd love to know what they said to each other," protested another writer on the panel. "Wouldn't you? The last words of someone dying..."

"Nope," I said. "We know the last words of a man who died at the top of Mount Everest in a storm. Jon Krakauer wrote about that storm in his book *Into Thin Air*, told us that the man had a cell phone with him and phoned his fiancée in New Zealand."

"What did he say to her?" asked the writer, her eyes sparkling.

"It's not so bad. I'll just rest here for a while and go on. I'm not cold."

"Oh." She faltered.

How writers write about what really happens, or about fiction, affects how we feel about what really happens. It can change our understanding of the personal and the political, it can change our work and our leisure and it changes the material world as thoroughly as it changes our hearts and minds.

There may be no completely effective physical barriers against bombs (whether military or terrorist). The only barriers effective in this matter are those in the minds of people: people who resolve to use the tools available to them, and use the tools well. How a person defines "well" is our most effective protection. There are believers in Islam who weep when their faith's name is grandstanded by killers, just as there are Christians who weep when fellow Christians shoot at or bomb abortion clinics. The tools available to Gandhi were the words and bodies of thousands of people, assembling without violence to protest the actions of a government – and these tools were effective because that government also intended to minimize violence. Now we have to be aware that the same materials used for bombs and weapons are useful as fuel and tools – they are integrated into our modern world.

Our best protection against the tactics of fear and horror is to make fear and horror unnecessary. When the hungry and homeless are safe, when the frustrated have an effective forum for improvement, there is less resentment. And that's a change we can make.

Dentist

I've had a couple of great days lately. Sure there's blossoms in the garden centres, and my peas are up and looking good. This year's experiment for the market garden: purple pod peas. Try saying THAT three times, fast, after visiting the dentist! And yes, some of the errands I've been doing included a couple of trips to the dentist.

It doesn't seem like such good news to see a dentist. But dentists have made me... happy.

Anyone who has seen the fantasy/Sci-Fi movie "Little Shop of Horrors" may be remembering Bill Murray's cameo as a masochist who begs a sadistic dentist for a long, slow root canal. "It's your professionalism I admire," he flirts when a mirror and a probe are distorting his mouth. That's not what I mean! Dentists don't make me happy like that. I just don't want to worry about my teeth.

I didn't use to think about dentists, except to get my kids in for checkups. But now the kids are grown. I flossed, and brushed my teeth with "sensitive" toothpaste and became very careful when eating hard things. Drinking hot drinks gradually became something I was so good at, it should be a spectator sport at the Olympic Winter Games. ("And now for the parallel Games," the announcer would say, "our next competitor is challenged with sensitive teeth and no sense of balance! There's the starting gun... Ooo, that must have startled her. She spilled all over her Team Canada uniform. Gonna lose points for that from the Russian judge.") It took even more care to drink something cold or eat a Popsicle – something I can't get through the summer without.

But when an old filling crumbled a while ago, I had to go for an emergency filling. And you know, that was better than the achy tooth had been. Another tooth that had been bothering me took me to a dentist again – and I had a root canal, done without all the fuss and suffering that others tell me they've endured. What was different about me?

Well, for one thing, I'd been eating well all my life, and had regular check-ups as a kid. I've kept up the habit of brushing and flossing all my life.

For another, after my dental work, I felt better. I hadn't realized how much I'd been chalking up my daily feelings to the weather, to a non-challenging job versus the pleasure of writing as a professional, to middle age or my hearing loss. But when my teeth were better, my whole life felt just better. Like shoes that fit. Like enough for dinner (but not Thanksgiving full). Like maybe I could do a non-challenging job or another one when the first went away, as so many do, and keep meeting my writing assignments as well. Like maybe I could grow older without crumbling apart as my old filling crumbled, or at least I might crumble more slowly.

It took a couple of relatives getting heart conditions before I learned that the same germs that cause tooth decay and gum disease also cause heart problems. When my dad learned he was going to have to have a cardiac bypass operation, the doctor sent him to the dentist first. Sometimes the damage is already done by the time the person goes to the doctor or dentist. My uncle worked overseas for a couple of years, and put off getting some abscessed teeth cared for until he came back to Canada. The germs got into his blood, and caused a stroke. He needed a heart valve replacement, too. It's taken him ages to get better enough to drive, and look after the house, and he's telling everyone who'll listen: take care of your teeth.

Any health care – body, teeth, sight or hearing – that comes through our provincial health programs is something that can only do all of us good. I don't mind that people on welfare get partial dental benefits – I wish it was full coverage and I wish everyone had it. When a stranger has no pain it makes us all healthier and safer. Keep those skilled professionals busy! My dentist has the hands of a fine craftsman.

So bring it on! Bring on the replacement for my old filling, or the crown on my bicuspid. Bring on a full cleaning, with the hygienist saying "How many years has it been since your last? Wow, have you ever been brushing and flossing right!" Because it doesn't take forever, and now that I have some benefits (at the current non-challenging job, for however long it lasts) it doesn't cost the earth. Because the lack of pain is a comfort in my life and for those around me – like a rising tide that lifts all boats.

Harmony

I once pulled a knife on an Edmonton bus driver – and he thanked me.
Using that sentence, I won a round of that game where a group of people each say three outrageous things about themselves, two of them true and one false. It's a good game for moving on from knowing each other slightly to being able to work together in harmony.

This group of people had already been working together for a while, and riding together on a municipal bus packed with commuters. Harmony is as harmony does, but after that game I heard a few more conversations going on in the back of that bus, and saw a few more drivers arrange for car-pooling their fellow workers. Social interactions are funny things, and it's interesting to see how people interact a little more thoroughly once they know each other's names and something about each other. Something outrageous helps, but something ordinary doesn't hurt, either.

Like the three guys I saw hovering near a couple of girls at the bus stop. Guys will always hover near girls who are young or pretty or both, and talk to them a little, maybe flirt a tiny bit. Guys will even hover near women who are no longer young or pretty. I asked my husband about that one day, and he said, "Oh, it's practise." He flirted politely with someone at our farmer's market table one day, and when I pointed out that he was married and she was a nun, he responded blithely: "She was a girl once! She might have a niece, or a friend. And how do you think I know what sort of things to say to YOU, my dear?" I guess my husband needs less practise than he thinks. At next week's market, the nun was back visiting our table, with a friend. Another nun.

What I mean to say is, guys will hover and give bits of their attention or lots of it to girls, shy guys as well as playboys. Even gay guys will hover near a friendly girl. And the three guys I saw hovering near the pair of girls at the bus stop were not gay. They may have been too shy to ask the girls out on a date, but the hope of it showed in the tall guy's eyes, in the short guy's stance, in the way the stout guy held his book. The fact that the statistical chance of a date with either girl was very low did not bother these guys – the odds had gone UP from zero, when no girls were around. That was what counted.

So I waited for the bus, and saw the shifting of male feet, and heard a few shy, cheerful words exchanged about the game we'd played earlier. And that was it for conversation, followed by a companionable silence, with me off to one side, being as nearly invisible as only a middle-aged woman can be.

And then the bus came, with two bikes on the front rack and a slew of Japanese tourists in the front seats with their tourist maps spread open. And the three guys pushed onto the bus ahead of me and the girls.

They clomped to the last empty seats at the back of the bus, and sat down. "I got nothing going for Saturday," one said to the others. "Yeah," said the tall one. The other held up his book.

It was no surprise to me that they had no plans for Saturday, but there was a confused, bewildered look in their eyes. I guess they may have had no clue why the girls chose to stand near the Japanese tourists instead of them. It was payday, the weather was sunny and somehow they'd just blown their slight chance of having a great Saturday at the lake with a few pretty girls. I guess an introduction to each other and a good-natured game to discuss was no substitute for a little practise in social interactions. Harmony is as harmony does.

Oh, and the game I'd won? My wisecrack about pulling a knife on a bus driver was no lie. It happened over a year earlier.

The bus stopped at a timing point, and I was the only person to get on. While the driver shut the engine off, I fumbled for bus fare. "Hey, you need another quarter," the driver told me, pointing at a large sticker on the fare box. The rates for regular fare, children, seniors and students were posted there.

I pointed at the top of the sticker. "I was reading the line here," I said. The new sticker had been slapped on crooked over the old one, and the top line was showing the old rate. The driver picked at the old sticker, but didn't have enough fingernails to get a grip on the edge.

"If you need something to scrape off that old sticker," I suggested, "I have a jackknife in my bag." I had to open the lock blade for him.

He used it to make short work of the old sticker. "I've had to tell people all day about paying the extra quarter. So that was why!" And he handed back the knife with thanks. It was only a small interaction, but a harmonious one.

Bracelet

So, there are these motivational bracelets that are one of the newest fashions. Somehow I like these better than wearing headsets hooked up to MP3 players – at first glance it looks like the listener has the earplugs hooked into nothing, A doubletake gives me the impression the earplugs are hooked into a cigarette, which leads to a third surreptitious glance at a little music player abut the size of my thumb. It's yet another technological wonder, but you know, I like the wonder that comes from realizing that motivational bracelets are now mainstream instead of marginal culture.

It's hard to imagine that instead of a granola-eating hippie writing "Believe" on a ribbon around her wrist, there are society matrons wearing bracelets to proclaim their belief that a cure for breast cancer is possible. Tough guys can now wear a yellow bracelet just like Lance Armstrong. And there are ever so many variations on the "What Would Jesus Do?" bracelet. You can play the game of "What would this famous person do in my situation?" or "What would this fictional person do?" and you can play it for laughs. Or you can play "What would I do in someone else's situation?"

It hasn't escaped my attention that at the same time my husband was giving my kayak a push so I could paddle around some shallow waters, there was another husband in New Orleans pulling his own wife along on a door floating on floodwaters.

I used to wonder what I would ever do in a disaster, and so I learned as many practical skills as possible and got St John's Ambulance training in first aid. Then in the winter of 1999 I was at my parents' home in Victoria when four feet of snow fell overnight. The skill that was needed that week was snowshoveling. Go figure. I'd been ready for an earthquake. What the city of

Victoria learned that week is that disasters are dealt with not only by resources in trained hands, but also by communication. And the communication needs to be not only among the trained workers, but among everyone needing and giving help.

The news out of New Orleans looked pretty bad at first, and then it got worse. I found it hard to believe that twenty thousand people could just stand outside a convention centre, waiting for someone to help them. They couldn't all be physically disabled, I thought. Are they ignorant of how to load a knapsack and walk to the next town?

I am ashamed to admit those thoughts now, after hearing even more news from New Orleans, and it's even worse. A friend of mine who edited a book on *The Architecture of Horror* has been keeping a website on the aftermath of Hurricane Katrina. Others have been writing of their experiences for internet websites, and the stories are more discouraging than what shows on television and radio and newspapers.

It seems that after 80% of the population evacuated New Orleans, most of those who left were either less physically able or else unable to afford travel to stay in another city. Some of the visitors trapped in hotels pooled their resources to charter buses to come get them, but the buses were commandeered by police as they arrived at the city. And people who were told by the police to walk over a bridge that leads to another city were met by an armed roadblock on the bridge – police from the other community would not allow them to pass. They didn't want another Superdome in their own city.

When there are so many police officers working hard to save lives and maintain peace, it is upsetting to hear about the officers who are confiscating food at gunpoint and the few who are organizing looting. When there are few technicians working to maintain what public utilities they can, it is even more upsetting to hear that the trained help arriving in New Orleans consists mostly of private security guards hired by the wealthy to protect their un-flooded homes.

And the people who are able to leave New Orleans on foot and by bus to an airport, they arrive in other cities and states as refugees. I've heard of one airport worker who gave her shoes to someone who had none.

It's been suggested that the cost of Hurricane Katrina could bankrupt the American nation, in insurance claims, damage to oil rigs and damage to America's largest port. I'd suggest that a national government that sends in Blackwater mercenaries instead of the National Guard is showing that they are already morally bankrupt. There is plenty of money in the USA. But assigning it so that people can eat and sleep and work in good health... that's another matter entirely.

After enough playing silly games based on motivational bracelets, it becomes clear that the real question to ask is not only "What should I do?" but also "Am I doing it?" Any bracelet on my wrist should be worn while working for health and strength together with my friends and neighbours. And I hope that I'd be able to give my shoes to someone who needed them.

Neighbourhood

E ver notice that you can learn a lot about houses, and the lives of people in them, by walking around a neighbourhood? Well, maybe not your neighbourhood. I've visited some places where house after house on road after road is built from the same material, with the same profile, shape and roofline. Clearly they were all built during the same summer. Sometimes I can look down a street and all I'll see is a series of double garage doors facing the road, and recessed to one side of each garage, a solid front door with a deadbolt lock and a security company's sticker saying "Armed Response." It's like a street where only cars live, and each car is holed up with a gun in case some human opens the door.

Can you blame me if I like better the houses that look like people live there?

Some houses show me what the people who live there do. The house with a basketball hoop out front, the one with a ramp added during a renovation, another with a pear tree trained to cover an east-facing wall – those are homes where people are living. I can guess at what happens there, even if when I walk by, there's no one out in the yard. And sometimes I can even guess at the interactions between people in neighbouring homes.

There are two homes among many along a certain stretch of waterfront. I went out in my kayak on that calm water, and paddled past one small, homemade dock after another. But two were side by side, and after looking at each for a minute, I could see that something was going on here.

There were two floating docks, ramps and boathouses side by side, almost exactly the same size. The docks and ramps were obviously the oldest parts; it looked like first one had been built and then the other next to it, so each family would have its own dock. Then a small boathouse was built by the first dock, and soon after that, the other boathouse.

Perhaps the second boathouse was a little fancier or more finely made. But the first boathouse was constructed from shiplap siding painted yellow and white in a style similar to the main house, which could just be glimpsed through trees and bushes from the water. The second boathouse was in covered in stucco in a more modern style than its own main house, a style that was already beginning to look dated, like any fashion does after a few years. For instance, the glass panels around the rooftop patio positively signalled "Five Years Ago" as clearly as the two padded lounge chairs.

By comparison, the rooftop patio of the first boathouse was an addition, but one that did complement the original construction. The white picket fence around the little patio matched the garden fence. And while the seating was only cheap, white plastic lawn chairs, there were four of them.

So! Looks like an on-going dialogue here. A pair of neighbouring families, speaking slowly to one another in the pattern language of their construction work. And what have they been saying to one another? Beyond "I am here" or "This is my place" – these two sites have been saying "I use this" and "I fit well here" along with a little bit of "I am spending money on my recreation."

Hard to tell if this was a discussion or a genteel argument. Was this a friendly contest? It may have been a conscious competition to impress each other as well as make good use of their waterfront properties. Unless I wrangled an invitation from one of them for a backyard barbecue and a cold drink on one of those rooftop patios, there was only one way to know if these neighbours were having fun or keeping up with the Joneses. I'd have to look at their boats.

Each dock had a rowboat turned turtle against its respective boathouse wall, surely the oldest boats. The stuccoed boathouse had a sleek motorboat tied up, and a kayak on the dock, a fibreglass model that looked like it was zooming at top speed while it lay still. The yellow-and-white boathouse had only two kayaks on the dock, made of rotomolded plastic. It was pretty clear who had won the contest of owning the most expensive boats.

But all three boats at the stuccoed boathouse were wrapped in tarpaulins, with a few dry leaves caught in the folds. And when I drifted closer, I could see the two plastic kayaks were wet. It was nine-thirty on a Sunday morning, and these people had already been out paddling and come back in time to get to church. Even their old rowboat looked like it had been moved recently.

Maybe I still don't know for sure who won the contest of having more fun. What do I know? I laid my kayak (ten feet long, plastic) on the shore next to other boats (fifteen feet long, fibreglass and handmade wood) brought by other people come to enjoy this shoreline park. I envied their boats. They envied my three outings earlier that week. Even the finest boat of all can only take you somewhere when it's in the water.

It is a fine thing, to own a good boat and to own a good place where you can enjoy your time. But it is even better to put the boat you have into the water, and to share your time with friends.

City People and Country People

There are times when it becomes more apparent to me that city people and country people are different. There are times when I suspect that there are deep-down, fundamental cultural differences which can never be resolved. There are other times when heartwarming moments at country fairs hold out the shining hope that all urban dwellers will honour and respect the fields that feed us all and the wilderness that gives us space for our teeming anthills, at the same time that all rural dwellers will honour and respect the drive that says "I'm going to make something interesting enough to talk about during and after work." Listen to the talk at a corn feast and you can tell that for once, everyone's having a good time. But mostly I end up where I've always ended up, with a foot in each camp and a hand busy in each kind of work.

You can tell some of the fundamental differences between city people and country people by seeing how they react to similar things. Like that highway nightmare of hitting a deer with your car.

A couple of years ago a neighbour had that happen. A neighbour, out by the farm, could be anyone whose acreage is anywhere within ten miles, someone who might wander up at an auction sale and ask where we got the Caution – Children Playing signs for the posts near our farm driveways. Those signs have the most appalling stylized ideogram of the front end of an '85 Buick knocking a small child and his ball into the air. Everyone who looks at the signs, shudders. The school bus driver loves 'em, and says that "Only a complete jerk could drive by that sign without slowing down." By that standard, we have three jerks living somewhere north of us on that road. But everyone else slows down, looks out for my nephews and niece and wonders where the hippies' kids are now that they've grown up.

One of those neighbours, on a dark night in early winter, had the highway nightmare. His truck hit a moose. After collecting his wits, the man walked home. He had to get another truck with a winch and a rifle to put the injured moose out of its misery (it takes more than a half-ton pickup to kill a moose). He also woke a relative to help tow the truck home (a moose is more than enough to kill a half-ton pickup) and to help get the moose home to be cleaned and dressed and cut up for the freezer.

Now, I know that according to Fish and Wildlife regulations we're supposed to report the incident and leave the carcass for them to handle. But I also know that no one out on the acreages would ever dream of reporting this as poaching. I think of it as practical.

Practical is not what I'd call the response to another highway nightmare, a couple of weeks ago. I've had a city job for some months, and carpool with a co-worker who gets me most of the way home. Walking the last mile at eleven at night clears my head after a day indoors. Talking in the car on back roads is a social thing, a way to get to know your co-workers, especially if an extra one or two comes along for the ride. But you haven't got to know anybody until you're with them in a car that hits a deer.

The driver reacted well to my comment: "Deer!" He braked and slowed so that when the little sedan bumped the deer, the collision wasn't bad. The deer somersaulted, got to its feet, ran away and leapt over a barb-wire fence. It was lost in the bush in a moment.

But after one understandably panicked squawk, the three other people in the car sat frozen and silent. I got out, leaving both men and the woman, all of whom are bigger and stronger than me. The deer was gone without a trace, and the bumper was undamaged. I got back in and told the driver his licence plate was a little bent but there was no other problem.

Never try to reassure city people that there's no problem by telling them that there's no blood left anywhere. That was when they started to shake. For some reason, they weren't relieved to know that I ran my hands around the bumper and didn't find any clumps of hair or skin.

The driver's hands shook as he put the car in motion. He didn't know what to do for the deer. We were close enough to the city that I said I'd call the animal control officer to report the collision, as the animal might be found injured nearby. But it looked pretty spry jumping the fence.

It was so upsetting for the driver. The other two chattered, trying to reassure him and each other. Nothing like this had happened before for him. He'd been upset even when his cat had killed a mouse. "Oh, I hope that never happens again," he said, of course. "I never want to hit a deer again."

"Or if you do, heaven forbid, kill it clean so it doesn't suffer," I said. "And hey, I'd clean and dress it so you could take it home."

Never try to joke with city people about cleaning and dressing a dead animal. It doesn't reassure them when you've scared them with the thought of what to do when an animal lies struggling in a ditch. That was when they got quiet again. It wasn't till then that they realized why I had gotten out of the car.

So, I'm not car-pooling this week as the driver's on vacation and the other two are riding the bus. But they still wave at me when we see each other at work, just like country people driving by and waving at someone on a tractor. Neighbours. It's good to have them.

Love

We are in the season to gather among friends and family and neighbours for a cup of cheer and armchair discussions. Armchair discussions that spring up in any season include the natures of war and love, and reconciling human needs and greeds.

Among the needs we all have are air, and water and food; and needed very nearly as much are the comforts of a safe home, where we take care of these needs for ourselves and those we love. There are many names for love, and many kinds of love discussed by armchair philosophers over late-night cups. Filias is family love; Agape, the love shared for one's brother in Christ. Eros is romantic love and Caritas is the love of our fellow humans.

Caritas, or the English word Charity, seems pale and watered-down after the fire of Eros, the lasting bond of Filias, or the fervor of Agape. Charity has a negative connotation for some people, separating people into categories like "worthy to receive" and "worthy because of giving." As if the worth of human needs or kindness could be counted like cans of condensed milk on a shelf!

When I'm buying that tin of condensed, sweetened milk for a holiday dessert, I'm going to donate another can for the Food Bank. That small act will not change the world, nor even me. It's not taking the high moral ground, either, if there is any high road. Ivan Illych, a Canadian writer, wrote that: "The day is coming, indeed it is already here, when a man who has two loaves of bread cannot sleep in peace until he shares one with his neighbour who has none. This is the low road to morality. There is no other."

Put like that, charity doesn't seem like something which separates people into worthy givers and worthy receivers – and nothing for the unworthy. Charity begins to seem more like caring, the other form of this word in English. Caring for one another can be caring for someone's needs, as a nurse tends a patient. It can also mean liking a person, and taking an interest in her or his well-being. And when I think of it that way, that pale, watered-down kind of Love called Caritas seems good as bread.

Without the intensity and the selectiveness of Agape, or Filias or Eros, what is Love? Is love something you can feel for anyone? If it isn't a unique, personal connection, is it love? Is it love that saves us from rage and despair and greed?

It is love when we grow food or build roads or do other work that touches the lives of not only our own family and friends, but people whose names we may never know. It is by love that the faithful and the infidel are brothers and sisters – quarrelling and jealous, perhaps, but united in common humanity. And when the hungry are fed, the naked are clothed, the sick are tended and the oppressed are comforted, this love sustains all of us as a rising tide lifts all boats. It unmasks preparations for War as acts of Hatred and Greed, not Patriotism and Defence.

This is a love that, though vague and impersonal, is broad and deep as the sea and sky that carry our commerce around the world. It can sustain us all like the air we breathe, like our food and drink. Though Caritas cannot bring us the personal pleasures of family, friends and faith, it is how we make our forum for these loves secure. And it brings tidings of comfort and joy.

Looking For A Sign

"That crow!" snarled my husband. It can be frustrating to see my hard work as futile. It certainly was frustrating for Bernie this fall, when he raked up a great big heap of leaves at my parents' house in the city. He piled the leaves at the curb. The municipal workers were due by in a few days to vacuum the leaves into a truck. Pleased with his efforts, my partner put away the rake. When he returned to the front of the house, there was a crow standing on top of the leaf pile.

The crow appeared to be finding something to eat among the leaves, perhaps bugs or other tasty morsels. The crow picked up leaf after leaf, turning each over and laying it down carefully ... on the lawn.

If there had been, say, a shotgun within reach, there would have been bits of crow, the crow's nest in the bare tree, and I daresay even the leaf pile scattered all over. Bernie made do with harsh language. "That rotten crow is out to get me," swore my partner.

It wasn't surprising. That crow is particularly bold, since my mother started leaving stale bread out on her patio for the birds. But then Bernie contributes to this interaction as well. This is, after all, the man who has been seen clutching a mug and a spoon and standing over a kettle as it comes sloo-oowly to the boil, shrieking: "Instant coffee! It's supposed to be INSTANT coffee!"

Well, for weeks now, Bernie has tried drinking decaf chai tea with milk and honey instead. I have to admit that crow gets to me, too. One of my homemade bread loaves failed, so I put it out on the patio where my mother leaves stale bread. But apart from one dismal poke, my loaf has gone untouched. Crows are getting pretty fussy these days – in winter, too!

My partner eyed another crow as we went for a walk yesterday. "I've decided that one crow putting my leaves back on the lawn was not some odd evil crow out to get me," he anounced.

"Good!" I squeezed his hand.

"Yep," he said. "They're ALL out to get me." He tugged me aside to avoid walking under a branch where the crow waited to dive-bomb us. It missed.

Just because I feel paranoid at times doesn't mean nobody is out to get me. Paranoia is something that strikes at odd moments and in odd ways.

There's an older fellow I know who has been having disputes with his neighbour. There have been regrettable incidents on either side, involving garden hoses and anonymous fluids on driveways... and I hasten to add, for anyone keeping track of older fellows or neighbours, that neither of these guys is related to me. Winter does not bring an end to their interactions.

The older fellow reports that his snowman has been broken apart in his front yard. It did no good to suggest that the snowman might have been kicked apart by kids passing by and goofing around. Nope! The older fellow assumed that this was the latest sally in his ongoing battle with the neighbour. "But I'll show him!" he crowed. "I had a stockpile of snow stashed in the back yard." After an ominous pause, he announced triumphantly: "And I re-built it!"

We can't always have a stockpile of snow ready in case of snowman vandalism. And I gotta admit, re-building a destroyed snowman is better kharma than hunting down various crows. When a fellow who's gone more than a bit dotty can come up with a better answer to his paranoid fantasies than I can, well, I know what my resolution is for the new year. I'm going to try to deal with random moments of paranoia with the snowman approach rather than the shotgun approach. It goes down better, especially with a mug of decaf chai with milk and honey.

Sign On My Forehead

Is there a sign on my forehead? No, not the wrinkles or the silver hair hanging into my eyes. I'm thinking there is some kind of sign that people are reading, one that says something like: "Talk to this person!"

I can't walk down a street without people saying hi. An old woman who glances fearfully at other people on a street corner will say "Beautiful day!" to me. The young fella who stared at his shoes when he passed the last five people will look at me and nod. Kids in strollers and dogs on leashes turn their heads and wag their tongues when I go by. Maybe it's my clothes or the way I wobble when I walk.

Sometimes the attraction is the knitting in my hands. The usual question is, "What are you making?" which often leads to strangers telling me about their own sweater, or hat or scarf. But little kids ask, "What are you doing?" When I say that I'm making a sweater, they look at me like I'm pulling their leg. "**Dis** is a **sweater**," one said, tugging on her fleece sweatshirt. Some kids have never seen a handmade garment, much less understood where polyester fibres, cotton or wool come from. "When you cut the sheeps furs off, do you have to hurt them?" When such questions get asked, somehow everyone in earshot is waiting earnestly for my reply. And then they tell me their own story.

One little old lady stopped her station wagon right in the middle of the road to talk to me. She rolled her window down and peered past my husband, who was taking me out for a morning pull. That's our current fitness activity – Bernie tows me around the neighbourhood before breakfast. For Christmas he gave me a walking stick. It's great when the road is slippery.

It was the walking stick that got the little old lady's attention. "Where did you get your stick?" she asked cheerfully, listened and nodded. She held up her own aluminum cane for inspection. "This is more of an indoor cane, for when I'm around my grandkids. My, it's a stormy day. I'm on my way to Cattle Point. I'll bet the wind is blowing the open water right up onto the path, there. But I've got my binoculars." She reached for and held up a fine big set of binoculars. "I love to go there and look for kayakers."

Bernie's hand tightened on mine. "Not birds?" he muttered to me.

"I look to see if any of them are out without life jackets. And if they come close enough, I give 'em what for," the sweet-faced grandmother said fiercely. "I wouldn't go out on a log without a life jacket, much less out in one of those kayaks!" Until that moment, I hadn't thought we had ever met this particular little old lady. But I realized that she or someone like her must have been among the shore-strolling people who informally inspect our kayak and gear every time we launch.

"Well, I should be going," she said brightly. "It's my birthday tomorrow. I'll be ninety-two." And she was off.

"Is there some kind of sign on our foreheads?" Bernie asked, as we resumed our walks. "One that says, 'Tell me your story!' Everybody talks to us." Around the corner, we were suddenly hailed by a tabby cat. It walked down from a house's front porch, along a footpath and right up to Bernie, meowing fiercely all the way. "Well, the sign works for cats, too," he said, and petted the cat as it rubbed against his ankles. "Hey kitty, are you like Lassie in the movies running for help and barking to say Farmer John broke his leg?"

"Definitely," I agreed as the cat walked back and forth, trying to lead Bernie to the front door. "She's saying: 'Hey, human! Get up there with your thumbs and do whatever humans do to make the door open!'" There was a note taped to the front door, which we didn't need to read to know it must say: "Hi Fred, came to feed the cat but couldn't find the key. Back later." If cats could work can openers, they'd never need to talk to us. But they still would talk to Bernie and to me, because of the sign.

I guess instead of looking for a sign from God to tell me what to do, I'll have to settle for other people seeing the sign on my forehead saying "Tell me your story." Because they've done it all my life, and you know, it's not bad at all.

Assisted Death

There's been two media circuses in the news that I read, but only one that I saw. While driving the other night near my parents' home, I saw red and blue lights flashing on the highway ahead, and took an exit to avoid the tangle of emergency vehicles of various kinds. On the overpass I went past a pair of police cars bracketing a sedan, and went on to drive home two young friends, about the age of my daughter. It was only later that I learned from the news that the sedan had been left on that overpass by another young woman about the same age, who had jumped onto the highway below.

Stories of this young woman's suicide were carried in the same newspapers that held news of another woman dying now in the United States. Depending on what you've been able to find out about her, Terri Schiavo is either comatose or responsive; she may need heroic measures to keep her alive in an unresponsive state or she may need only food and water and nursing care. I couldn't tell you what the truth is, only that her husband and her parents disagree about whether or not to remove her feeding tube, and that there are judges and doctors and lawyers who have been party to this decision for most of the years Terri Schiavo has spent in hospital.

There are politicians and spokesmen and demonstrators gathering to make their opinions known.

I don't know what that young woman thought, when she parked her car on the overpass only a few yards above the highway. I don't know if she looked at the sky, or at the outline of the low mountain nearby, with a road right to the top of a cliff much higher than that overpass. I don't know if she chose the overpass because other people have flung themselves off overpasses in Toronto, but the news has never carried a story about anyone committing suicide off Mount Douglas.

I don't know what pain or despair led her to choose suicide, what she was thinking. But I'm guessing that she didn't think that it would take two cars to kill her. Or that the second car would be driven by another young woman nearly her own age, a young woman who had recently lost both her own parents and was now the guardian for her teenage brother. Or that the young brother would be the passenger at that horrific moment.

There are people who speak eloquently and fiercely about suicide, and the morals or ethics of their beliefs. I cannot pass any judgement on the pain and despair of the young woman who suicided. But I can have an opinion about the contagious cruelty of suicide by neighbour, which inflicts so much suffering on someone who has no choice to avoid it, no awareness of the impending collision.

And I can add that the crowning touch for this media circus was when the car insurance company told the young driver that she would have to pay a $300 deductible, that she would lose her safe driver discount, and that she could not have the use of a loaner vehicle while her car was being repaired. It took a public outcry for ICBC to retract part of that judgement, but she still has to pay the $300 deductible.

While the media circus still goes on around the hospice where Terri Schiavo slowly starves to death, her parents quietly went home for Easter and suggested that others should spend that time with their own families.

Preparations

Early spring is a time of preparations. Some of the birds are moving already. The weather patterns are different from winter. And standing in the sunlight is no longer like getting a blood transfusion – something vital and necessary but thin and scanty compared to the healthy pounding heartbeat we expect.

Spring makes my heart pound! Partly from warming, because the sunlight actually has the power to warm me when walking along a country road or standing at a bus stop. Partly from chill, because I refuse to wear my winter parka any more. Still, I carry a toque in the pocket of my light jacket, so I'm prepared for a cooler turn in the weather.

I'm trying to get prepared for other things as well. Come summer I want to go paddling on the North Saskatchewan River with some friends. Long days on the water are no fun when someone gets tired out quickly, so I'm trying to build my cardiovascular strength. Walking a few extra blocks between bus stops doesn't seem like much, but getting my pulse pounding for that few minutes does make me brighter for the rest of my working day. And it means that all my blue jeans are mysteriously looser and baggier now than they were at Christmas – wonder how that happened?

I'm wondering how to prepare for other things that I know are happening. My brother's new job means he'll have no time later this spring for a short holiday – we'll have to put those hopes off till fall. My sister-in-law's taking her family to Europe – does that mean they'll need a house-sitter? And there are other preparations less cheerful, for events that are approaching at the same pace: one day at a time.

Our cat looked unwell, so we picked her up and inspected her drooly mouth. Why, she'd lost a tooth, and her jaw was swollen! Off she went to the vet, only her second visit in thirteen years since she was spayed. Our sister-in-law, who is also a vet, couldn't be reached; she has kept the cat tuned up with yearly immunization shots and worm pills and during one hectic phone call talked me through dosing the cat with ipecac to purge all the mouse poison she'd found.

This time our cat's health could not be remedied by a shot, a pill or an apology for her ruffled dignity. Her jaw wasn't swollen from the lost tooth – the tooth had fallen out because she had a tumor on her jaw. Whether it was the fast-growing or the very fast-growing kind was not an issue. Her days were numbered.

It's foolish to take too much concern over a pet when there are so many things going on in our lives and the world, things that we can improve and maintain, things that we can make better. But even when we couldn't make our cat better, we could make her comfortable.

My mother was the only person the cat would let wash her drooly chin. "I think she knows I'm being gentle," said my mom, who is taking medication for the lingering pain of shingles. "She purrs afterwards."

For weeks, my father has been sharing his morning coffee and newspaper with the cat on the quilt over his lap. But he put his quilt aside on an electric heating pad to make a warm nest for her to sleep most of the day. "She wants a warm place, this or a sunbeam," he reported. "Winding down." The cat woke him up one night, tapping on his pacemaker battery. Must've been looking for a warm place to sleep, tried to curl up on his chest and wondered what the hard thing was.

Bowls of dry cat food were no longer our cat's diet. This cat used to pay the rent for years in mouse heads lined up in the porch to be admired – she deserved soft food, whatever kind she would eat. And she got her choice of various flavours until it was clear she wasn't really able to eat more than a few licks.

So our cat has returned to the elements. When spring has warmed the fields, our grown children will bury her ashes on our farm, where the cat explored Nature and her own feline nature. After adding another small mound of earth and stone to the corner where pets are laid, the twins will walk out to the place where my grandparents' ashes are put, among rocks piled up when this land was cleared. This farm has been under the plough for a hundred years now. The biggest changes that can be seen are the ones renewed every year. Old houses disappear, iron rusts, but young trees only grow where the plough doesn't disturb them every year. And overhead, the migrating birds circle and lift on the rising air warmed when the field is ploughed, black, in spring.

Agenda

I'm coming up to several deadlines right now. Spring is one of the big ones, and you know what that does to your daily schedule. Each morning you look out on the new day and there's always some change, like Daylight Savings Time. Is it going to be warm today? Is the frost in the ground going to thaw this year? Maybe it will rain enough to pull warm water down to melt the frost. But then, when will the ground be dry enough to run a tractor over the fields? Sometimes in spring there's no telling what work will be done until the morning's weather is certain.

Of all the seasons, Spring is not some sweet, innocent baby. It's a young teenager. It wakes up some mornings loud as a robin in the fir tree asking "Hey! What's to eat?" It bangs around the house, turning everything up loud and eventually stomps off into the day with shoes bigger than anyone expected. Other mornings you can't get Spring out of bed with a crowbar. "I'm awake," Spring mutters, and pulls a sheet of snow over its head. I found Spring half-way up a tree and couldn't decide if it was a kid or a professional arborist. "Gotta get that branch off. I'm under deadline, you know. Move it, move it!"

These days I work with teenagers a little older than Spring, at a call centre. We had a deadline the other day, learning to work with new computer programs. The guys who come around to help when I have trouble ordering a new phone for a customer, well, most of these helpers are young as my grown children. Of course they learned the new programs quickly – they never used the old ones. (Old from a few months ago.) And they do marvel at how customers almost never get angry at me, unlike the rest of the call centre workers. Well, of course customers rarely shout at me! It would be like yelling at your auntie. Only a real creep would do that. By that standard, a couple of creeps a week call me – and most of them interrupt themselves to say, "But I'm not angry at you, you're trying to fix it and can't. Get me your supervisor who can be yelled at."

I've got other deadlines, too. I'm working on a couple of books for an educational publisher. One is on AIDS. That's scary, the idea of teenagers slipping into a school library and reading my book so they can learn what they need to know about AIDS. I have to hit the right tone, writing like an enlightened, non-judgemental older sibling giving advice to a younger sibling. But every time I get some statistics from the United Nations to put in the book, I keep seeing some kids with weird hair reading my book so they can say to their moms, "I can so get a tattoo without getting AIDS! I read it in a book." And I want to tell them to pull up their low-rise pants and shampoo their hair (purple dreadlocks are fine when clean) and... well, I better get back to that enlightened, non-judgemental advice.

What makes me an expert about talking to young people anyway? I don't have any magic technique. Aside from remembering not to stare and laugh when they tell me they don't have a driver's licence. What is it with not driving these days? When I was twenty the only young people I knew who DIDN'T have a licence had some emotional problem as well. Apparently insurance rates are a big factor, but that's no barrier to getting a licence, only to getting one's own car and insurance.

But I digress. And I've got deadlines. And other goals, like writing to my 14-year-old neice to congratulate her on getting her learner's permit. First try! So I'm going to take my statistics on AIDS with me to work on at the bus stop and between ordering new phones on a computer program that only works when I stand on my left foot. There's a robin in the fir tree by the bus stop, singing loud as Spring, with an agenda of her own.

Having Fun

Did you ever wonder what animal has the most fun? There's a couple of candidates that come to mind. Dogs are clearly the front runners in this contest, if not the winners.

If you don't believe me, you don't know dogs. They do whatever they're doing with their entire attention. Eat, scoot around, get dirty – they're always having fun. They even have fun when they're napping.

I've never seen anything nap as intently as a dog. The only time I ever saw anything come close to that single-minded determination to nap was after nursing my twins when they were babies. They had naptime down to a science. Scoot around getting grubby till someone cleans you off and rubs you down with a towel. Eat with a hearty appetite, then curl up and fall deep asleep with a sigh. Maybe my kids were puppies in an earlier life, or were really in touch with their inner dog. At any rate, they still know how to have fun. My kids grew up, but they still give dogs a run for their money in the contest of who has the most fun.

A friend of mine suggested ducks have more fun, but I have to disagree. Ducks are fun to watch, I admit. And ducks do duck down and stick their tails up in the air at whoever is watching, which looks like so much fun to do that I simply have to try it sometime. But when ducks are going places, take a gander – er, a peek at what's going on. If they're swimming, they look calm and cool above the waterline, but below the surface there's a heap of flailing going on to keep them moving.

When they're out of the water, things aren't much more fun. They waddle. It's hard to have your dignity when you waddle. (Trust me, I waddle. It's true.) And it's hard to hold onto your sense of humour when you've lost hold of your dignity. It must be like carrying two suitcases, one in each hand. And ducks waddle as slowly as if they each had two carry-on bags and were headed towards the luggage carousel at the Airport. "Got a cart?" one quacks. "Who, me?" quacks the other. "Your turn." They quack with every step.

You'd think ducks would have more fun when they're flying. But ducks have migrated over our farm since the Ice Age or before, and I've heard them talking to each other. They're happy to be strong, and to feel the updrafts from a ploughed field, but they're counting cadence, not telling jokes. The second duck back from the point man at the head of the vee is not saying "Didja hear the one about how many humans does it take to change global warming?" She's counting off: four more! Three more! Two more! Some ducks fly low enough to land in our field or dugout pond. There's always a lot of noise when they land or take off, more than you'd think two ducks, or maybe four, could ever make. But one of them is quacking: "Get an early start this year, you said. Be ahead of the crowd. There was ice on last night's pond! And there isn't even any duckweed growing in this one." Nope, ducks are fun to watch but they're not always having fun.

The animal that is both fun to watch and is pretty much always having fun is the otter. I've been watching them. Otters have a good time all the time. They live where lots of their food grows, so unless an oil tanker runs aground nearby, life is like one endless frat party where the pizza and beer just keep turning up whenever you're finished playing Frisbee. They sleep in a kelp bed, which is more comfortable than a waterbed and no worries about leaks or having to get up to go find the bathroom. And they play all day long.

I heard about some kayakers paddling out among islands and kelp beds in Desolation Sound. One sea otter comes up close to a kayak and starts looking cute. You know what he must have been saying with his friends a minute earlier: "Watch this, guys, I dare ya to bump his rudder!"

The paddler stops, pulls a rubber cover off his hatch and begins fumbling around for his camera. Has to get the shot of a lifetime, an otter right beside him!

The otter steals his hatch cover. Takes it off into the kelp bed. He's still playing Frisbee with it, for all anyone knows, laughing it up with the guys. Meanwhile the kayaker gets some great photos but still has to paddle two hundred miles to Prince Rupert with a plastic bag and a rubber band over his open hatch. Otters have the most fun, way more than ducks and even more than dogs. No contest.

Vacuum

If you're ever looking for a line to stop a party in its tracks, you could try what Louise came up with at her potluck nacho-making party this weekend. "Where do I get rid of a vacuum cleaner?" Louise asked. And with that, everyone in her apartment fell silent.

It was a question I've never been asked before. Where DO you get rid of a vacuum cleaner? The dust bags are easy: just throw them in the trash. There's no point in trying to empty the bags out and re-use 'em. I've tried, back in the past when I had more dust than dollars and would occasionally run a vacuum cleaner even though the sound of the motor can give me a migraine within minutes.

Now I have dust and fewer migraines since I never run a vacuum cleaner. "I've never gotten rid of a vacuum cleaner. Why are you getting rid of this one?"

"I've got a better one," said Louise. "This one is just getting in the way." It was sitting in her living room, next to her couch, like a potted philodendron. Most people decorate with end tables, lamps, and so on. Louise is different.

"You could give it to Value Village or a thrift store." Bernie shrugged. "Does it work?"

"Nope. That's why I bought a new one."

"You could take it down to Goodwill," suggested Stephanie. "They fix things and sell them in their own thrift store."

"Used to. They don't any more."

Huh. So how could she get rid of a vacuum cleaner, a non-working one? Couldn't just put it in the trash bin – it would fill the whole garbage can. "I put it next to the garbage can," Louise said. "But it was still there after my trash had been taken away."

She couldn't put it in the blue box, not even the plastic casing because it didn't have that recycle symbol pressed into the plastic. It began to look like her boyfriend John was going to have to smuggle it out into the back of his van tonight, and drive out to the dump to get rid of it.

It wasn't toxic waste, or a murder victim, it was just a worn-out vacuum cleaner. There had to be some easier solution that didn't feel like we were taking it out into the middle of a lake somewhere to sink down amid the fishes and the ooze. That would be bad.

"Does the vacuum cleaner repair shop take old ones?" John wondered. "Tell them: 'Here, you can have this. Fix it, sell it, give it away, throw it away.' Then it's not your problem any more."

"I don't think they'd want one this old. Too old to fix properly."

"I never have trouble getting rid of things," said Stephanie, who lives on a moderately busy street. "I just put them out on the boulevard with a sign that says FREE and they're gone within an hour or two. I got rid of two old computer monitors that don't work and two old CPUs with no hard drives and no modems that way. Put a sign on 'em that says DOESN'T WORK, FREE and they're gone."

"I've got some old computers I'm bringing over to YOUR place." My partner Bernie grinned. All we can usually do with old computer components, though apparently they're well worth recycling for the bits of gold and silicon, et cetera, is let our son strip them for material for his art projects.

"Oh yeah, I can usually get rid of anything with a FREE sign," said Louise. "But this already sat out all day beside the garbage can at the end of the driveway, and nobody took it. I don't think anybody around here wants it. That's got me baffled. Usually, leave anything out and it's gone. Once, I had to get rid of an old mattress from an apartment where I used to live. My ex-husband rented a truck to haul it down to the dump, and I carried the mattress down to the back alley behind the apartment building. We went out the front, got in the truck and drove around to the back alley, but the mattress was already gone. Renting the truck cost more than buying the mattress had in the first place."

"You could go to somebody's yard sale with your old vacuum cleaner," said Bernie. "Put a $2 tag on it and when nobody's looking, leave it under the table."

"I like how when people are tired of selling things, they just leave the rest by the curb with a FREE sign," said Louise.

"That's another opportunity to leave the vacuum cleaner, in with all the FREE stuff," said John.

"Yeah, but what if nobody takes it, and it just sits there for a while?"

Then inspiration struck me. "You could put it on somebody's doorstep with a note that says "Please look after my vacuum cleaner.""

My partner nodded. "In a basket, with a blanket." Clearly, Louise's problem was now solved, but now she was the one staring blankly at us. The moment could have gotten awkward, but luckily the oven timer rang, announcing the nachos were ready. Problem solved.

Nice

Everyone who owns a boat of any kind should also have a working knowledge of cardio-pulmonary resuscitation; not because boating is so dangerous, but because it's a useful talent that may be necessary when you didn't expect it to be.

Well, not just boat owners. I'm one of those people that thinks you shouldn't be allowed to graduate from high school without a St John's Ambulance certificate in Emergency First Aid, which includes training in CPR as well as what to do with cut arteries, compound fractures and small objects in ears or noses. (What does one do? Oddly enough, for all of the above the answer is "Go To The Hospital" – but after getting the certificate, you know which of these doesn't require calling an ambulance.) Heck, I believe that if you don't know first aid you shouldn't be left at home alone, much less allowed out on a snowmobile or in a boat.

On the farm, we became acutely aware of just how far it was to the nearest medical help. Redwater is 20 minutes away if you drive at 120 klicks on washboard gravel and pavement, Morinville about the same but all pavement after the first mile, and when both of those centres close the nearest is Sturgeon Hospital in St Albert. And yes, we've ended up en route to medical care at odd hours of day or night, driving with one or the other of the twins keening in the passenger seat. Is it any wonder that both my partner and I have first aid training, and our bathroom first aid kit has Benadryl, topical spray anesthetics and LOTS of clean towels?

This summer I prepared mini-kits to carry on our kayaks, and gave one to my friend Louise. "I've already got a first aid kit in my hatch," she said.

"This one fits in your life jacket pocket." I showed her the film canister, holding two Band-aids, the head of a Bic razor to shave off jellyfish tentacle stingers, and six tablets: two Advil, two Pepto-bismol and two Tums.

The week before, Louise had gotten two blisters and I'd had a migraine with nausea. Plus we'd paddled past a red jellyfish, the kind with tentacles that sting like wasps. "I'm ready for anything!" crowed Louise. But it's been ages since any of us did CPR, so we're all getting refresher training. And it's not just for emergencies when we're in isolated places, or on the water.

If you tell someone about your boat – anyone at all, not just someone who also owns a boat, or wishes to own a boat, but absolutely anyone – if you tell someone about your boat and he or she does not say "Hmmm... Nice." ... check that person's pulse.

I'm serious.

When being told about your boat, everyone will say "Hmmm... Nice." (Or the cultural equivalent, which may range from "Dude, that's sick!" to "I say, smashing news!") It doesn't matter whether they wish they had boats of their own and so say it with envy, or if they already have much nicer boats and so say it with a condescending tone. Even if they never in their lives wanted a boat, they'll say it with sarcasm.

But if someone doesn't smile and nod when you tell about your boat, check that person's pulse. He or she may be dead.

If not, that person has the social graces of a Galapagos tortoise. Don't take him or her out in your boat.

And you know, it's pretty much the same when it comes to snowmobiles or motorbikes, sewing machines or barbecues, computers or kite-powered dune buggys. All stories about our new toys get the "smile and nod" response, even if the person isn't really happy to hear about your new toy. Perhaps that smile is because the person is actually thinking: "Yeah, I remember when I got MY toy." More likely, it's just a social grace, like holding a door open for someone.

And I think that's fine. Much as I like Galapagos tortoises, I don't want one in my boat. It's not about scaly feet scrabbling on the gunwhales, it's about social graces. Part of being on the water means that I'm not within arm's reach of the yob who stood too close to me on an elevator the other day. And part of telling people about my boat is the smile and nod I must give while they in turn tell me about their cats, or trip to Vegreville, or recipe for barbecued corn on the cob. Hmm... Nice.

Schooled

Hard news, to hear of another school shooting, this time at Dawson College. And once again, the shooter was not a berserker pushed suddenly over the edge to run amok with bare hands or whatever weapon came to hand. Once again, the shooter took time to gather weapons and go to the school.

Fifteen times since 1975, someone has gone to a Canadian school with a gun and an agenda. And that's not even counting the time in 1977 when my high-school principal was knifed by a former student in the school parking lot. By the time the shooter begins to fire, there's usually not much anyone can to avoid multiple injuries, death and suicide by cop. Usually the shooter is a student.

When it's an adult, he's not able to be steered from his crime, because of chronic mental illness and long-term distress. One Canadian school shooter was a husband unable to adjust to a divorce, another a professor who didn't get tenure. The male pronoun is used on purpose here, because almost all school shooters are male. Chronic mental illnesses take a while to fester, and are usually due to multiple causes.

But when the shooter is a student, the acuteness of his mental illness is usually a response to the student's experience at that very school. And from this fact, I draw some hope. If we improve the experience for most of the students (if never absolutely every one of them), we might make shooting up the school seem less possible.

We've already learned how to prepare schools for these emergencies once they do happen. General emergency preparedness helps cope with fire or earthquakes as well. At Dawson College, everybody reacted absolutely right. The students ducked and ran, helping each other escape. The teachers were alerted and instantly decided whether it was right to evacuate the room immediately, or lock the door and bunker down as well as possible.

The police have learned through experience that it's best not to wait for the SWAT team, but engage the shooter immediately; they drew his attention and fire. The nasty event came to an abrupt end about four minutes after the first shot was fired. The careful search for any possible accomplices was both necessary and thorough.

So, we've learned how to prepare schools for these emergencies. Now, what we need to do for our schools is how to help the students have better experiences at school. It may be one of the determining factors in making school shootings less likely. And if not, well, there is no excuse for any school tolerating bad socialization among its students. There is certainly no reason we should accept bad socialization as a major or minor factor contributing to school shootings.

Where mental illness is due to genetics or diet or personal trauma, it has to be treated on a one-by-one basis. But where frustration and lack of social connections and loneliness are factors, we can improve those for almost everyone in a school. From an institution's zero tolerance policy on bullying to an individual's effort to smile and share pencils, we can each improve social interactions at schools. It may not have seemed worth insisting on, for the one-third of students who leave Canadian schools with lingering emotional scars, or the few who commit suicide (how many last year?) If we do it to reduce the chance of one in a million students coming to school with a gun and an agenda, we may not reduce school shootings to zero – but we will definitely improve school experiences for many students.

"It can't happen here!" students were heard to scream as they fled Dawson College. That denial is natural. But we have to learn to deny that these things can happen, not only where we are, but ever. Our instant, natural protest has to become the one that says this event just can't happen at all, not just that this danger can't happen to me.

Being Prepared

I've been thinking again about preparedness. Yes, I know too much thinking is a bad idea. Yes, I know this is the season to hang a Venezuelan cotton hammock between two trees and lie across it in the shade. Preferably with a big cold drink and some fruit. But that would require being prepared with a hammock, water and fruit – and actually being near some trees. So some thinking ahead is a good thing.

It never fails to amaze me how many people don't think ahead. That's how some ordinary days can become a problem. A day at the beach ought to be a party, but it can become a great, big, hairy deal.

Out on the coast near my parents' place is Nanoose Bay, and just the other day, a Navy ship was cruising into harbour when a crweman spotted something in the water. It was three teenage boys clinging to a chunk of styrofoam.

They'd gone out in an inflatable toy boat with a couple of friends and visited an island a mile offshore. But on the way back, the toy boat lost pressure and sank. They were lucky to find a floating piece of styrofoam, broken off some dock in a recent storm. And after only half an hour in the cold sea, they were glad to be rescued.

It was a close thing. Another half-hour and any or all of them would have died from cold, or drowned. Their friends on the island with the other toy boat weren't happy when the Navy ship loomed over the little island, and the boys were told in no uncertain terms to Get Aboard The Navy Ship. A little planning would have kept that day at the beach from becoming a problem.

Officers become understandably unhappy when solving other people's problems on the water. But there's a staff sergeant in Ontario who is a very happy man this summer.

Up until recently, anyone convicted of boating while impaired, in Ontario, was banned from boating for three months. It had not escaped the staff sergeant's notice that this was hardly a motivating punishment for offenders. By the time an offender was convicted, it was usually December. Banning someone from boating in January, February and March – in Ontario – doesn't have much effect on that person's behaviour.

But this summer is different. This June, a private Member's bill went through three readings in their provincial parliament and was signed into law the same day, in an unprecedented show of non-partisan support. Now, anyone convicted of boating while impaired will lose his or her DRIVING licence for three months.

There is a very happy staff sergeant in Ontario this summer. He's not jumping on the odd fisherman with one beer in his kayak, or kids getting a little too far from shore. But he's confident that when a day at the beach becomes a great big hairy deal, he can enforce the law with a little more back-up from the legislature and the justice system.

Talent

You never know where your talents will lead you. Some people have one particular talent; some have a number of abilities in various fields but no genius in any of them. And sometimes you can find a moment when you do something a little unexpected, that brings an unexpected pleasure.

I don't have one particular talent. In the absence of genius, I've made a sincere effort to develop moderate abilities in various fields. You've heard the saying: "Jack of all trades, master of none"? Well, I prefer to pitch myself as a jackknife, and on good days a Swiss Army jackknife – one of those with two blades, a screwdriver, bottle opener, can opener, awl and scissors. You know, the kind of jackknife you can't get through airport security anymore. Heck, you can't get a pair of boots through airport security these days without taking them off for the X-ray machine, let alone carry aboard a little pocket knife that's almost as sharp as the ones the flight attendants hand out for meals in First Class.

But I digress. Yes, I'm a Jack of all trades, a jackknife person capable in several different fields. So is my partner. So are some of our friends, who I've taken to calling my "Focus Group" when quoting them for my publishers. When editors ask me to do market research for my science articles or health books, I run the ideas past my Focus Group. When pressed I come clean: the Focus Group consists of my twenty-one-year-old offspring and their friends, my associates with an average of 3 varied careers each, and my partner (who can chat up damn near anyone and learn damn near anything).

So when we get together, what do we do for fun? This time, we stumped an expert in marine biology. Completely.

Y'see, we've been messing about in boats for months now. Back on September 12 we were kayaking in a quiet inlet, and came across some floating jelly balls, about the size of a golf ball. Looked rather like an egg yolk, but transparent and no colour. Lots of them were lying on the muddy sea bottom. We got pictures for our website (kayakyak.blogspot.com). Couldn't figure out what they were, in spite of our interest in the natural sciences. One of the paddlers asked a biology student what these jelly balls were, and got a referral to a real scientist.

This man has one of those single-track careers. He's in charge of the Invertebrate Collections in Marine Biology at the Royal British Columbia Museum – in plain language, he collects and keeps track of sea life that doesn't have backbones. He's a world-class expert on marine worms and other sea animals. And when we brought him a couple jelly balls in a container packed in ice to keep cool, we caught him flat-footed.

He'd never seen one before.

For anyone who hasn't been to Victoria, BC, I can confirm that the weather is mild enough that in any month of the year you can find not only amateur science buffs like my friends paddling around in every single ocean bay, but the odds are good you will also find a professional fisherman and a couple of university students as well. In the home waters of a world-class expert, in an inlet that's been under continuous human use since the last Ice Age, we found something new.

To give him credit, this was worse than bringing in one tiny red berry and asking a horticulturalist to describe the tree it came from. Chokecherry? Huckleberry? Edible or poison? We should have scooped up a couple gallons of mud from underneath the jelly ball.

It's taken six weeks of him e-mailing photos to pick colleagues' brains for our expert to come up with the guess that our jelly balls are the egg masses of a polychaete marine worm that lives in the mud. He can't even tell us yet if these bristly worms are the kind that look like giant millipedes or the ones like giant wood lice or the others like feather dusters. But if he hasn't figured it out by March, he'll be asking questions at the International Polychaetes Association conference in Maine. Yes, there's an international association of experts in bristly worms – I can't make this stuff up.

And now you know how universities and museums spend their money. Not only do they collect items for display and research, not only do they make time to answer casual questions like this from fumbling amateurs, but they have conferences every few years where experts at observing the natural world get together. Not only do they talk about what they've seen, they talk about what it means. It was at a conference like this, over a few beers, that biologists realized that frogs around the world were badly affected by the thinning ozone layer.

So a weekend discovery by a couple of jacks-of-all-trades may give some experts the information they need about how Global Climate Change is affecting one area, and one species. If we hadn't been paying attention to the wildlife around us, we might never have noticed these unfamiliar specimens. And if my partner hadn't worked as an environmental technician, we might not have been able to take a usable sample. And if the expert didn't take time from his lunch hour to look at it, well... You never know where your talents will lead you, or the unexpected pleasures you might find.

Lights

I like the lights that get put up this time of year – white and coloured, bright or blinking, from casual to contrived. There are driving tours or recommended routes marked out in some newspapers, but I don't follow them. I prefer to see what goes by if I'm driving or on the bus at night. Sometimes I borrow a dog and go for a walk.

You see more of a community on foot. In vehicles we go through a community or past it. In vehicles we each keep to our own boundaries, cordially sharing a road or bus seats but politely refraining from too much interaction, boxed in a tonne of metal and glass.

My December tours are on foot by choice, or sometimes by bicycle. Oh, I don't mind passing the odd farmhouse that's lit up, visible from a long way off as I drive down a country road. But when I set out to look at lights, I go where the houses are closer together, and I go at a slower pace. Slower than my partner, that is, who rides a bicycle at breakneck speeds and whose long legs eat up the ground at an incredible rate. I will walk only so fast; if he wants to go faster he can go on ahead and I'll catch up eventually. If he really wants me to go on at his pace, he can tell me so and take my hand.

It may look romantic to passers-by, who see us walking hand-in-hand after twenty-four or twenty-five years together. But he's towing me along as we go.

And we do go for walks, with or without a borrowed dog or two for an excuse. "The human needs the walk," says my brother, who at one time had three dogs and was outweighed by their combined mass. "You take a dog out because, well, the dog HAS to be walked. But humans need the walk at least as much." And while the dogs are sniffing everything from knee-height down to the ground, and reacting to every windblown leaf as if it were another deer leaping from behind a bush like one did last month, the humans are looking around and up. These days, we're seeing a lot of lights.

Oh, not every house is decorated for the festive season. There are mostly plenty of dark places with a front door huddled under a forty-watt light bulb. Candy Cane Lane has some appeal, when the weather's good and you can mosey along on foot. But dotted here and there along sidestreets, or on a bright corner with a lot of traffic, there are some enjoyable festive light decorations.

I can't call them all Christmas lights, because that's not the reason for all of these lights. Some of the decorations are decidedly secular and opulent and non-religious in nature. Also, I saw a menorah in one window. And there's the house where one of many local Hindu families lives, who painted their house a cheerful orange (in a neighbourhood where the prevailing opinion appears to be that there are only two acceptable colours to paint a house, white or brown, and only a fool would paint a house brown). They've lined their path and driveway with lights reminiscent of the little lamps used for Diwali, the festival of lights. They've also hung a large aluminum foil star over their door, perhaps from some ecumenical urge to adopt a Western festive image that's not overtly religious. Alas, the star is hung with the point down. But their hearts are so clearly in the right place.

Then there's the house I first noticed when Bernie and I were newly-married. It had rows of coloured lights along the roof ridge and chimney, as well as the gables, gutters, windows and porch. Fifteen years later, the lights detailed only the gutters and bay windows and porch. This year, there's a single line of lights all along the porch handrail. I think that gradual progression isn't from a change of owners, but shows the light-hanger's aging from second-storey man to man clinging with one hand to a ladder to man shuffling along a porch.

Another house I passed by has a postage-stamp lawn clipped like a military brush cut. "Ooh, look, someone got a bit happy," I pointed out, and pulled the borrowed dogs away from sniffing at the single, artistically pruned little tree with a line of tiny, multi-coloured fairy lights wound around it.

"Someone got a bit TOO happy over here," Bernie said at the next house. It didn't look like too much to me: lights along the gutters, a couple of net lights draped over shrubs... then I saw the two parallel ropes strung between a poplar and a birch, and hanging jauntily between the ropes were strings of lights wound around wires twisted into the shape of reindeer. Swinging in the breeze like laundry. Um.

You know, rather than any of these decorations I'd choose any day the star my brother-in-law welded out of iron bars and strung with red lights. Taller than me, it hung for years high on a grain elevator near the highway. Everyone saw it, coming west. Neighbours knew it was his. Anyone seeing it knew it was handmade to fit; an emblem of peace made from strong materials, pointing into the dark sky.

Weather

Weather... happens. Weather is what happens to you, while climate is what keeps happening to everyone.

It never ceases to amaze me how many people can go outdoors and be gobsmacked with dismay at the weather when it's an ordinary seasonal day. Where did they think they lived? I'm not talking about tornadoes or hurricanes here, just ordinary weather that might happen any season of the year and particularly the season we're having.

And I'm not talking about times like when a bride I know woke up to find she couldn't be wed outdoors under a blooming cherry tree, but must be married indoors because the blooming tree was bowed to earth under the weight of a snowstorm in May. No, the cheerful aplomb of that bride was admirable, as she wore boots for the brief walk between car and door, carrying her shoes and the hem of her wedding dress high out of the splash zone.

I'm talking about people heading out from home on an ordinary mid-week day, who can't walk a block without getting wet feet and chilled blue. It's half-past January, people! Anyone who got a new parka for Christmas and isn't wearing it is just not paying attention.

My daughter started work in a high-end sporting goods store this fall, and marvelled at the racks of expensive parkas with fur-trimmed hoods. "How many people would ever pay $400 for a parka?" she wondered, until the first cold snap hit. −15 Celsius saw a steady stream of customers shivering in business suits or hoodies. Many were facing their first cold, snowy winter.

They didn't want ski jackets. In Canada, when you overhear a man in a sporting goods store saying he wants it to hang to his knees, he's talking about buying a winter coat. Show him the windproof parkas with long sleeves and fur-trimmed hoods. Technical insulating fibres work, but they don't show their warmth like fur-trimmed hoods do.

Even my son, who puts together his own goth/punk clothing from pieces of various black garments, even he dresses for winter. He's cool, but he's not cold. In our family, we all agree: It's not how long your coat is, it's whether it covers your butt.

And as far as wet feet go, some people forget about fashion and take the solution a friend of mine summed up in three words: "Zellers. $8.99. Gumboots." With a pair of wool socks, it's one way to have warm, dry feet.

Others are lucky. I walked into a shoe store this winter and found Sorels on half-price. In my size. Broke the budget, but well worth it. One of the store clerks helped the trainee ring up the sale, telling her, "Waterproof to here, felt-lined, warm and comfortable, best thing for winter. I wore mine to a wedding last year."

I wore them on a walk with my husband the other day. Usually he takes me out for a brisk pull as he tows me along, but it was an icy, slushy day so I guess we were out for a teeter instead as I got to set the pace. We walked past someone teetering herself on spike-heeled shoes more suited for a dance floor. "There goes one young woman who puts entirely too much trust in technology," muttered my partner.

"Yeah? Well, I trust in it, too," I said. "I trust my gear."

"Not the same thing. You prepared yourself for a variety of weather conditions. She's counting on snowplows to clear her path." When I slipped a little on the ice, he helped me regain what little balance I have. "You want to take the bus the last bit of the way? We've got that steep hill ahead."

"I bet you ten dollars," I snarled, "that you fall and I don't."

Well, there were a couple little slips for both of us, but yeah, when we got home I had to give him ten bucks. And now it's time to get a box together of things to donate to the shelter, the one that gave a friend of mine clothing coupons for their thrift store, to get a winter coat so she apply for a new job without looking like a ragamuffin. Weather is hard on people who didn't get a new coat for Christmas or find winter boots on sale. And climate is what's happening to everyone, whether I notice it or not. With the way that climate has been changing over the last few years, I'd rather be part of the preparations than just count on snowplows.

Paddle Naked

He wasn't wearing a stitch of clothing. But all I could see of my partner's skin was a narrow band from his eyebrows to his beard. "I'm all geared up!" Bernie announced happily, slapping his sides.

His new sleeveless wetsuit was a Christmas gift from his sister, and it clung like a second skin, under a nylon paddling jacket. The cold weather cap I gave him for Christmas made his head look like a black, sleek egg. His paddling gloves were pre-curved neoprene. His feet would stay warm, if not dry, inside short neoprene boots. With a nylon skirt to seal around the cockpit of his kayak, and finally a life jacket over it all, I could only guess at the contours of his body.

He was the least naked man I've ever seen who wasn't actually wearing any clothes.

"Clothes" is defined, of course, by the gold standard: You Can Wear Only REAL Clothes When Visiting Your Grandparents. If you can't wear it to your grandparents' house, well, it's not proper clothes. Talk to any teenager if you need a definition of real clothes for that purpose. But what you wear while kayaking has a different purpose.

We go kayaking to feel the wind and water, like kids playing on a log at the shore. We want to get closer to wildlife, and to feel the liquid muscle of the sea lift our boats and bodies. I've become used to the taut feel of my own short wetsuit, and annoyed at the awkward feeling when bending at a waist thickened by the wetsuit and a neoprene spray skirt. Some people look sleek like an otter or a seal in neoprene. I look like the Michelin Man.

It's hard to feel close to Nature when encased in petroleum products. But I admit, wearing a wetsuit can make all the difference between living and dying even when we're only a quarter-mile offshore. It can take five or ten minutes to turn a kayak right-side up, tip much of the water out of it, and scramble back in. One of our neighbours takes his own kayak out three times a week and he swears that spending twenty minutes in the water is all it takes to chill his hands into useless lumps. As for what he wears, well, if he's ever found mugged in the alley behind Smuggler's Pub and rolled for his Gore-Tex drysuit, do NOT ask me what I was doing at that time and if I have an alibi.

Even if I never tipped over and had to roll or do a wet exit, a wetsuit and spray skirt are good to keep me warm and almost dry from splashes in winter weather. But in summer...

In summer, some days are heavenly warm. When the water is glassy calm, when I'm in familiar waters, and within a few feet of shore, I'm willing to swim even in seawater only a degree or two warmer than in winter. It's time to paddle naked.

Well, as naked as society and safety will allow. Clothing-optional beaches are pretty much always a long walk away from a road, carrying a kayak. But wearing only a bathing suit – or tank top and bike shorts – seems pretty naked compared with a wetsuit. Bare feet on the footpedals feel astonishingly bare, and bare hands grip a paddle with more immediacy (and blisters) than when gloves are worn. I feel amazingly limber when my life jacket isn't buckled over a wetsuit and thin merino wool sweater.

It's not worth cheating on safety. Even in summer any lake doesn't get very warm, and the ocean never gets warm except for the ankle-deep wading zone when the tide comes in. When sea kayaking, paddlers need safety gear and should wear wetsuits, or dry suits and ideally have a friend hovering nearby in a helicopter with a SARtech and a winch.

But on a flat water paddle, in familiar waters safe enough to swim, it's good to paddle naked. No spray skirt to seal me into the boat. Bare feet, bare hands, bare arms and legs, sometimes I even go without a sunhat if the day's not too hot. It's a good opportunity to practise wet exits – otherwise known as falling out of the boat and scrambling to climb back in. Out with friends in their boats, we practise rescuing each other and try just one more time to see if we really can learn to roll back up after that disorienting moment of inversion.

It's hard to admit that it's not just the wetsuit that makes me look like the Michelin Man, it's having the finely-honed body of a freelance writer (limber hands and well-developed sitting muscles). It's been a long time since we were kids playing on a log at the shore. But somehow, I can still see the kid in each of us playing in our boats and our gear, even if that's all that can be seen in the narrow strip of skin between eyebrows and grin.

Manual

It amazes me how so many people can be so unprepared for some events to happen, modest problems that aren't extraordinary but are actually rather likely and should honestly be expected. What do you do, just give up when something goes wrong? A better choice is RTFM, as the computer programmers say, or "Read the flippin' manual."

I used to be baffled why so many useful devices break down so easily. Sure, with cheap ballpoint pens the reason is obvious: moving parts made from flimsy materials. But aren't computers made carefully? And why should cars break down so easily? My toaster is still doing its job after eight years.

RTFM! The toaster's manual was four pages long, and that included the warranty. The car came with a fifty page manual, and at Canadian Tire my partner picked up a detailed manual 150 pages long. Lots more moving parts in a car, and they move a lot more than a toaster does. Besides, that sliding lever on my toaster is kind of wearing out and you have to slide it just right.

I had a hard drive crash the other day. Computers just plain do that after a while. Run a couple of computers for a couple of years and dang, one of the hard drives will just up and stop working. All the files you saved in its memory are now gone. It's annoying but not as unexpected as it would be to have your car engine just up and quit on you. Usually cars make sounds that alert you to the wearing out process.

It's also a lot easier to deal with than a car. Cars have to be towed, and there's the whole decision thing about whether to fix it, or sell it for peanuts and start collecting pop bottles so you can save up to buy a bike. Computers, on the other hand, are small enough to haul over to your guru who takes out the useless hard drive and replaces it with one that has twice as much memory but costs about what you paid two years ago. Then you take your back-up memory and copy the files into the new hard drive.

No problem, if while saving those important files in the first place, you knew enough to make a spare copy and save it someplace else. As it turns out, even making a back-up copy wasn't enough for me during my recent hard drive crash. Two of my back-up disks are about five years old, and dang, they aren't readable any more. What actually paid off for me this time was having a paper print out of all my novel manuscripts. Manuals on How To Become A Writer always say to make two spare copies of all your stories and store them in two waterproof boxes. RTFM: swap one box with a buddy. That way, if either house should burn down, we only have to rescue people and cats.

Not the end of the world, or a national disaster. Just one of those things that happen. Some people fall apart at anything that's the least bit out of the ordinary. Others blithely blunder away from everything they know and out into the wide world.

Like the two guys who went out for a day hike in East Sooke Park near Victoria a while ago. Sure, they didn't grow up in that area, but even visitors could read the map on the sign in the parking lot. They went out on the wide, shoreline trail that runs over headlands and down into gullies. Time passed, and the two guys didn't get back to their car before dark. They spent the night in the rain forest, not daring to move in the dark, and terrified that they were absolutely lost. They lit a fire and didn't dare leave it to find more wood, so they burned their clothes, their shoes and their wallets.

Daylight came eventually, and they were found shivering, but well. The two guys were not somewhere in the midst of the dense, trackless woods where anyone can be completely lost ten feet from the road. Nope. They were both huddled over the ashes of their fire, in the middle of the two-metre wide hiking trail less than a hundred yards from the parking lot. When discovered, they asked "Are you the search party?" Nope. They were discovered by a family with a pack of little kids to wear out on the trail before going to Grandma's house for lunch. RTFM! Read the flippin' map, guys, when a map is there for you to read. You think it's embarrassing when a ten-year-old shows you how to use a DVD player? It's way more embarrassing to be rescued by little kids when you've burned your clothes.

RTFM helps when preparations help before a problem occurs. I'm not talking about dealing with a catastrophe. Part of the definition of a disaster or a catastrophe, as near as I can tell, is that events blow away most or all of your preparations. RTFM helps when thinking helps during a problem. God help us when tornados or earthquakes or the like make it hard to think at all.

Bees

Busy as a beehive. It's a proverb, and like most proverbs, it's easy to see why people say that. Check out any beehive – from a respectful distance! – and there'll be a constant motion of bees inside the hive. In the warm part of the year, there'll be a constant stream of bees flying to and from the hive. Well, most hives. Here in Canada, anyway.

This spring there have been empty hives in much of the United States. It was a mystery for the beekeepers: the winter bees that had lived some six months were supposed to be becoming more active in spring. This is when they raise a new brood, then enter the last three weeks of their lives, making honey and gathering pollen. But instead, the bees have been leaving the hives, not in a swarm to find a new hive. They've been going out alone and not coming back.

We raised bees on the farm, a couple of years, and it was fascinating to watch the hive. I still like to see beehives stacked at the edge of a field, and I still use local honey. So when the empty hives began being reported, it caught my attention.

There have been sudden deaths in hives before this. The verroa mite can get into a hive and cause all the bees to die. It's easy enough to understand that bees, being fairly small insects, can't support parasites as easily as we humans can get along with a case of fleas or lice. But it's not easy to understand why these bees have died and their hives are empty. They don't have mites. And while some of the live bees tested do have a variety of disease germs, the dead bees near the empty hives don't usually have more, or even as many germs.

There are a couple of theories. The first is that the bees are starving because pollen from genetically-modified food organisms (GMO) just isn't as nutritious as they need. The empty hives are generally found where the majority of crops are GMO. Another is that the bees are affected by agricultural spraying of weed-killers and pesticides, even as mild as the B.t. sprays to kill gypsy moths. The hives serving organic-method farms are less likely to be affected. And the newest theory is that cell phone calls are confusing the bees.

Well, I know cell phone calls confuse ME. With my wonky ears, I can't tell who is talking, anyway, resulting in such charming conversations as, "Hi, this is Paula." "Hi, honey, it's me." "Me who?" "Me, your mother. How many mothers have you got?" "Muggers? I don't want any muggers!"

It can only be more confusing for bees. "Hi, this is me. No, I'm not the queen. I'm the one who found the red clover before? Well, I found white clover next to the red clover. West of the hive, go about a hundred yards, it's kinda starting to rain a little." And they communicate with smells and wiggles. Wonder what the radio transmissions do to little tiny bee brains. Wonder if cell phones should carry a warning, like the one that says to minimize use by children, but instead says to minimize use while baby bee brains are growing.

There have been tests, with cell phone equipment of various kinds inside and near hives, and when bees are taken a short distance away, they can't find their way back. Sometimes. Was it the bee's first flight? Do the radio transmissions affect them more at certain parts of the summer bee's six-week lifespan, or maybe at certain parts of a flight? Or is it maybe that there are more cell phones and towers where there are more people, and therefore more car exhaust and chemical sprays? Maybe a number of things interact all together to affect a bee's ability to resist germs.

Humans and bees have been co-operating for a long time. We're even learning to understand some of their needs and the way bees communicate with each other. But this has beekeepers flummoxed. And they're taking it really seriously, because without bees to pollinate most crops, a lot of food simply won't be there for us.

So when you see those buzzing insects this summer, don't just lump the wasps and hornets in with the honeybees and bumblebees. And if you feel you simply must use a little poison spray in your yard instead of pouring vinegar on the weeds growing in your sidewalk cracks, well, read the label and follow directions. There's no excuse. It's not just honeybees that you'll be helping, it's butterflies and songbirds as well. And the people who make your yard busy as a beehive in summer.

Shell Game

D id you ever see that game with three walnut shells and a pea? It can be played with three cups and a little ball, or any similar set of objects. The idea is that you watch someone put a shell over the pea, and move the three shells around. Keep track of their movements! And then, guess which shell is covering the pea. If you're right, you win.

It's apparently one of those street gambling games, like three-card monte, that sharp operators set up on city sidewalks in order to coax tourists into betting money and losing it. I say apparently because I've never seen one of these games taking place on a sidewalk in any city I've ever visited. All the people I've seen setting up on sidewalks to earn a little money are playing musical instruments, juggling, or selling drawings or handmade necklaces. No hidden pea, no guesses, no gamble.

These aren't sharp operators trying to cheat you out of your money. These are small-scale entrepreneurs offering a small entertainment. Either you like hearing "Jamaican Farewell" as you wait for your bus, and toss a loonie into the instrument case, or you don't. You actually see the juggler and his little dancing dog, no guessing. Maybe you pick out a hemp macramé bracelet for a buck, or you walk on by. Even some of the beggars pray for passers-by, and sing out cheerful thank-yous.

One of these shabby entrepreneurs had set up on a Toronto street corner with a hat and a cardboard sign saying: "Little Grey Men are stealing my brain. Please give me money so I can hunt them down." I'm not sure what was going on there, but it wasn't a shell game.

I'm not always sure of what's going on, but I'm getting wary of shell games. From time to time, I see a couple of them going on, or the equivalent game of "Hey rube, think you've got this figured out? Wanna bet?"

I try to keep up on the news: read a couple different papers every week, listen to CBC radio, spot-check the internet. The fun part is seeing how one event is reported in different media, perhaps over a couple of days. Sometimes one reporter tells the story from a very different angle, because of interviewing witnesses or tracking down owners and so on. But when the exact same words are used in different reports by different news agencies, over and over, that's one tell-tale sign that many someones are writing their news reports with a press release in one hand, and not doing research. The same story gets passed around radio, TV and newspapers like identical walnut shells being slid around and around. Stories like how the RCMP now has a new commissioner, one who doesn't come from their ranks. For a while, there were two comments being repeated about that appointment, saying "he won't know how they get things done," as well as "a new broom sweeps clean."

Then there's a new piece of news, about how the censored parts of the Maher Arar report have finally been released, and what they revealed. Check it out. Funny, how the man in charge of censoring that report is now the new commissioner for the RCMP. Guess that shows what kind of broom they wanted, and what kind of sweeping is going to get done. Learning things like that feels like finding the pea under the shell.

The core of the shell game idea is that you can't win, not even if you try hard. It isn't enough even if you watch like a hawk when the walnut shells get moved around. The pea has been palmed and hidden. It just can't be found, no matter how well you look and keep track – well, it won't be found unless the sharp operator wants you to find it once in a while. That way you'll keep playing the game. And when you decide to stop playing, well, there are plenty of other people who haven't figured it out yet.

Jury Duty

This time of year is the turning of the year for many people – for farmers, harvest home is approaching and the end of the growing season. The school year starts in September, but even people who finished school long ago still remember that feeling of starting new projects in the fall. And it's amazing how few elections are ever scheduled for this time. Afterwards, certainly. Before, possibly. But between Labour Day and the Equinox? Not going to happen.

There's already enough happening. Stores are gearing up for sales – bookstores in particular do half their business between Labour Day and Christmas. Public works crews are out making hasty repairs to roads and facilities after a summer's wear and tear and before winter weather makes the ground miserable to work. Out in a quiet inlet in Victoria, the city sent a spokesman to corner a man who had built an odd boat a year ago out of scrounged materials – sort of a catamaran/rowboat. He's been sleeping on it in a quiet bay near a city park, and well, that apparently wouldn't do. Even if he did tidy up floating litter and clean up the beach area, sleeping outdoors is frowned upon.

The city of Victoria has been passing bylaws banning sleeping in parks, and asking the police to increase their patrols. It's unclear why it was so important to make this man remove his boat from the inlet right now. But even more, once that decision was made, I'm wondering why the city's spokesman didn't help him transport his boat to either of two sheltered bays where free public mooring IS allowed. Maybe he was busy. The boater certainly is, dis-assembling his boat and carrying each homemade part to trash bins or a friend's garage.

Laws can be funny things. There is no law with teeth that doesn't do grief to somebody. Edmonton has a law against sleeping inside City Hall; it's meant to discourage homeless people from coming into City Hall to warm up in winter or cool down in summer. I've been nudged awake by a commissionaire during a public concert, and I hear the commissionaires have gleefully administered similar nudges to councilors during meetings. The chief commissionaire keeps track of commissionaire behaviour, and those who deserve a reward are scheduled to serve at council meetings for the privilege of gently waking the mayor and saying "no one is allowed to sleep in City Hall." The administration of the law sometimes does get our attention.

For some of us, the only time law and order really hits home is when we're called for jury duty. I got the summons, and showed up September 10 with some seventy others. You could tell who had some idea how they might be spending the day or the next week or month: those were the people who arrived wearing tidy clothes and comfortable shoes, with a book in hand. Others kept taking cell phone calls, right next to the sign asking for all cell phones to be turned off in the courtroom. And still others kept turning in circles, looking as flustered and unhappy as if they were the defendants in the trials for which these juries were being selected.

One young woman asked to be excused when her name was called. "I'm a student," she explained. Into the calm, polite silence of the courtroom, she added, "It would interfere with my studies." "My dear," said the judge, "Jury duty would interfere with anyone's occupation. It is a duty of all citizens." She was not excused, but the defendant's lawyer challenged her, and she went back into the pool. She'll have another chance to be selected at the end of the month, when all of this group who didn't get selected for this trial come back for another selection day.

I didn't get selected either. But for a few minutes I was part of the process of holding a fair trial, part of the system that tries to determine what to do when someone is accused of doing something so wrong that attention simply must be paid. And you know, I hardly had an interest in the book I'd brought or going through my notebook to check my schedule for the next few weeks for the course I'm teaching and the course I'm taking. I certainly didn't doze off, waiting there, and I'm notorious for nodding off in concerts, libraries and even on buses till the rough ride through a construction zone wakes me.

I'm looking forward to going back at the courthouse at the end of the month, to having another chance to serve on a jury. Not that I'm looking forward to hearing about a bad event, or learning about some stranger's life; I just want to do my part in the process that says everyone deserves fair hearings, not just those who can afford to pay officials to take an interest in what happened.

It will probably cost me no more than two autumn days out of my life. And it's worth it. To look at a defendant and know that there's every reason to expect a fair trial, that due attention is being paid to the accusation, and that a bullet to the head in a back room is less likely in this country even than the surprise testimony of the cast of a popular TV show on forensics – well, that's worth a great deal. I feel glad to participate in this small way, and probably more glad than the commissionaires in Edmonton's City Hall waking people who doze off during free public concerts.

Mistakes

On Thanksgiving weekend a weather front came in from the Coast. Weather fronts are like insect larvae. It's hard to tell exactly which kind of bug is going to mature from a wriggling larva. You can never know exactly what the local weather is going to be like, so you have to know what you would do in any weather. A mistake in preparations when you're out for a walk means getting soaked in rain or having an umbrella blown inside out. A mistake when you're out on the water in a small boat is much more risky; but in our kayaking paddle group, both the most daring and the most timid have repeated the morbid joke, "It isn't a mistake if nobody dies."

My partner Bernie doesn't make mistakes on the water. He went paddling on Thanksgiving Sunday to practise handling his kayak in a stiff breeze. I carried some of his gear down to the beach (we live a stone's throw from the water in Victoria) and saw him off, saying, "Paddle safely!"

That's the same advice other paddlers were giving each other in Howe Sound, near Vancouver, that day. My partner paddled safely, and returned. But two of the other paddlers in Howe Sound didn't make it.

Bernie went out to Chatham Island, knowing to take care. When the tide is right, the current in Baynes Channel runs like a river. If there's wind blowing opposite to the current, it makes a series of standing waves. One of our neighbours who paddles three or four times a week calls that current the freight train.

The good news is that the wooden kayak Bernie built can handle those waves just fine. The bad news is that the kayakers in Howe Sound must have made mistakes, by the definition of our black-humoured joke. "It isn't a mistake if nobody dies."

It seems like these people were extremely fit, healthy and adventurous sports enthusiasts. But even all their experience and strength wasn't enough when the wind crested to 80 klicks or more, and the waves reached seven feet or so. The group were wearing only sports tights instead of wetsuits or drysuits. The paddlers in Howe Sound left an island, going out into rough water. The conditions probably became abruptly even worse as they went on. Two of them didn't make it to shore on the mainland. Two went to hospital for hypothermia. And four did the best they thought they could.

It's so easy to second-guess someone else's mistakes. But part of why my friends talk before, during and after our outings is to second-guess our own errors, laugh at them where we can, and learn from them.

We have been so lucky. Part of that is absolute luck when the weather changes or the currents are a little stronger than we expected from reading a chart. But a big dollop of our luck is being prepared. The first part is wearing a life jacket, or personal flotation device (PFD). As we gradually began paddling in more challenging places than a small, sheltered lake, we each carried the gear needed for safety. Safety gear (rope, pump, paddle float, spare paddle, light, whistle, air horn). Cold water clothing. Drybag with clothes, food & mini-stove for a hot drink. Compasses. Cell phones and marine radios.

Those paddlers in Howe Sound faced the same weather front Bernie did, but local conditions, as forecast, made the waves much higher than Bernie faced. I don't want what happened in Howe Sound on Thanksgiving Sunday to happen for my group of friends – or anyone else, frankly – and I'm trying to figure how it would be less likely. The big difference that comes to mind (after ensuring each paddler has proper gear) is simply not setting out from shore into rough weather. Camping on the island overnight should be an option, even if one's drybag holds only the most minimal camping gear: dry clothes, space blankets, granola bars and the wherewithal for hot drinks. Come to think of it, that minimal camping gear should be in every car trunk. It was in ours when we lived in Alberta. Most of it's in our vehicle now, except the mini-stove which is in my drybag.

Our group talks on shore and during an outing about how each of us is feeling. Mostly we're saying "Wow! Did you see that otter?" but also, we admit our fears and injuries as small as a blister. When luck is a factor, you have to bring all the best luck with you. My paddle partner brought planning, preparation and strength to his modest challenge. He wore a wetsuit and paddle jacket under his PFD. He was in familiar waters and familiar conditions. He modified his route to suit the weather. His boat was stable and under control. Between one wave and the next, he had the time and control to reach out and pick up one floating insect larva among many wriggling beside his kayak. He came back not only alive, but excited.

Doing the best you can is more than just trying hard and being brave during an unexpected challenge. It's also bringing the best preparation you can to whatever you do, and making an informed, reasonable estimate of what challenge you might face.

Makes You Think

"There's always something new," said a friend, when we were paddling our kayaks on Sunday. That day we were kayaking on a familiar, quiet inlet where we had paddled three times already this year. It's a sensible place to plan an outing when the weather report alternates between "cold and clear" and "snow." It's hard to get lost in a familiar place, and it's hard to get dangerous winds in sheltered waters.

"You do the same things in the same places over and over, and you think it's going to be the same old thing," said my friend. "But if you look for it, there's always something new, something to make you think." The new thing for this outing was a thin skin of ice, that broke in sheets and plates when our kayaks skimmed over and through, screeching and roaring on the rough edges. Our paddles crashed instead of splashed through the veneer of ice, where fresh water from little streams had frozen over the salt tide as it rose. Makes you think, about Inuit hunters. Makes you think.

You know who are looking for new things, who keep up on what's happening, who can always find something to make you think? Janitors!

My friend says janitors always know the news because they've got all the newspapers; maybe not first thing in the morning, but when they go round tidying up other people have left behind newspapers. Any television in a break room or radio on a cleaning cart is usually tuned to the news and talk shows. And time spent doing simple, repetitive work is time for careful, slow thinking.

Now, janitors know things – sensible things – about time and management, about repetitive duties and how to do them well. Janitors know there's no point in mopping the front hallway if the front walk hasn't been cleared yet of snow or mud and leaves. Janitors notice that flies are more likely to land on windows and tables where someone has left greasy fingerprints.

Janitors have a practical understanding, shared with dishwashers, that you can work as hard and as thoroughly as you can, but three hours later everything you have cleaned and put in order will have been dirtied again through normal, expected use.

And it was janitors who talked with me about the Polish immigrant who died at Vancouver airport. These were immigrants and the daughters of immigrants, who had been through Customs and knew airport procedures in Canada as well as in countries where guards armed with machine guns are an expected and active part of airport security. They were the ones who identified what had happened as an airport problem, long before the RCMP were ever called.

"You come off plane, they read your passport, they know who you are," said one cleaning lady. "I don't read much English, just newspapers every day. But I see there is investigation needed. Airport security knew who he was, why tell his mother he wasn't there? Why not get the employee who speaks Polish and Russian? Should never have been need to call police."

She had the insight that comes from going through Customs, not once but several times, as one of hundreds of people being handled in an orderly fashion. She understood keeping her passport ready and answering the questions that Security must ask, or may ask, or might not ask. She knew what it has always been like to travel in most countries, and even in North America now: that there are secure rooms in airports and travelers may be kept there for hours or days, where politeness may be the order of business or it may not.

Investigations are proceeding into that dreadful death and the events leading up to it. I wonder how many of us, after nine or ten hours of detention without communication and explanations, would find anger breaking through the veneer of calm patience we try to maintain when dealing with anyone official.

I have been a janitor and an office worker, taking pride in keeping things and people and information orderly. I have been a security guard too, as hilarious as it was then and as it sounds for anyone who has seen me lately, standing five-foot-one and with the finely-honed body of a freelance writer. But that was a long time ago. These days I go out in my boat a lot, looking for peace and that veneer of calm patience, whether I go alone in quiet and familiar places or go with friends to face new challenges.

We look for new places to go kayaking, and we learn from going to the same places again and again. Sunday's paddle taught us about going out on thin ice. The ice screeched and roared as the rough edges broke and scraped under our boats, startling ducks and geese into flight, and even a hawk turned its head to look.

Life Pro Tips

I've been thinking lately about issuing people copies of a manual. We get manuals with our cars, our cell phones, even our toasters. How about a manual for getting along in life? That's one I'd read cover to cover. That's one I'd like to hand out to people in general and annoying people in particular.

I'm sure you've met someone who clearly needs a few pointers on getting along in life. You've probably met more of them than you want to remember, and each had a handful of knowledge gaps that very definitely needed to be filled with useful knowledge. But I bet some of them had some of the same knowledge gaps, because I sure keep running across people who need the same advice or the same swift kick.

What advice would you give a person on getting along in life? It should probably be short and to the point. I don't really want to have a long, detailed conversation with all of the people who make it screamingly obvious that they need to read a manual about getting along in life. They've probably already had enough of my attention anyway. And besides, a manual is supposed to be more helpful than watching me jump up and down and turn red in the face.

So here's some pointers from the manual on getting along in life, based on suggestions from people I've been polling for the last few weeks.

Use your turn signals. If you can't use them properly, it's much too hard for you to handle driving a car or riding a bike.

Push the pedestrian control button when crossing at crosswalks. Really.

Drinking Dos Equis beer (or any alcohol) will not make you cooler, especially when you use a bendy straw.

Brush your teeth.

Go to a library at least once a year. And while you're there, read a book at random from the New Books shelf.

Put your trash in the trash, recycle and compost as much as you can, and put empty bottles neatly where bottle collectors can get them.

Clean clothes: not just a good idea.

Be nice to people with babies and little kids – quit scowling at them even if the kids are squalling.

When you open a door in a public building, be ready to hold it open for someone else.

Work makes you feel strong, capable, and effective. It can also wear you out, whether or not it earns you a living.

When choosing a job, remember there are more choices than an eight-hour shift with three hours spent commuting. A four-hour shift that's a twenty minute walk from home has positive aspects, like time for working at home.

If you can't make food, clothes or shelter, you'd better know where you're going to get them from and be nice to the people who make them for you.

Learn a word joke and a little game that's suitable to play with kids. You don't have to be a clown, just be able to play a little.

When watching sports on tv, don't say anything while the ball is in play. I'm embarrassed to admit how old I was before this really sank in. As my daughter's boyfriend explained after something she said made him miss the season ender for the Oilers: "This is not relationship time! Not during the game!"

Be willing to let somebody do something nice for you, especially if it makes them feel good to share or help you.

Be willing to do something nice for somebody.

If you think you've done more for other people than they're doing for you, get over it.

Whatever else you choose to wear, spend the money it costs to get good shoes – ones that don't make your feet hurt.

Special pointers for University students: If you're majoring in wearing black clothes, don't take a minor in jaywalking at night. Also, remember, everybody else does not have Reading Break or Exams the same time as you.

And for older people: Get your sight and hearing tested. And find out if there's anything to do about your chronic aches and pains. Don't say you don't have problems, or you don't care, or it doesn't matter.

Eyeglasses, hearing aids, comfortable shoes and pain relief go together like the four food groups. We have the technology. We have the resources. And after you get yours, do your part to make sure everybody else who needs them get them.

So it's a start, anyway, even if this isn't an entire manual. I'm sure you've got your own list. And while you're whittling away at it, have a happy new year.

Plans

It's been an interesting week for accidental connections. I watched *Away From Her*, a Canadian film about a man coping with his wife's descent into Alzheimer's, which deserved a couple more Oscar nominations than it has. I spent the weekend doing outdoor winter sports with a couple of friends young enough to be my own grown kids. And I planned a funeral this week.

Two funerals, actually, for my parents. They're not dead (and no, this isn't the set up for the old dreadful joke from Monty Python). They're pre-planning their funerals so that as many of the decisions as possible are made ahead of time. It could sound depressing and morbid, but it sure didn't feel that way at all, doing the planning with them.

This is pretty much what happens in the early part of *Away From Her*, with its beautiful images of the husband and wife cross-country skiing, and their tracks going off in different directions. The husband has to learn how to let his wife make the decisions that she still can, and the wife decides she'd better get adjusted to the long-term care facility while she can still decide to make the move.

This is actually how my dad organizes a lot of things. If he can't make bad news not happen, and he can't schedule it for the most convenient and appropriate time, well, he can ruddy well be in charge of how he handles it.

This is pretty much what happened when his sight began to fail. An eye doctor told him that age-related macular degeneration was going to make it harder to read and eventually he would have to stop driving. Dad has been a real team player since that diagnosis. He made a plan. He read all the pamphlets he was given, and because of them he knows to wear sunglasses when outdoors and to take vitamins. He now has several magnifying lenses and a bright lamp next to the chair where he likes to read. My brother got him a book of large-print crossword puzzles, and makes large photocopies of the newspaper's crossword for him. My grown kids made sure to come visit. And for a year, Dad drove attentively, aware that he had to be extra alert.

Six months into that year, Dad told the eye doctor he no longer drove at night. The doctor praised his decision, saying, "Your vision isn't so bad yet that I can't let you drive at night. But if you choose not to, that's good. It means you're paying attention to how you see. I bet I won't have to tell you when to stop driving – you'll probably be the one to tell me."

By summer time, Dad would toss my husband the keys to his truck on rainy days. He only drove on the brightest of days that summer. He just didn't feel right, driving on cloudy days. And at the eye doctor's office, he learned that his vision had deteriorated much faster than expected, and he shouldn't drive any more. "You were right," the eye doctor said. "You could tell." And he shook Dad's hand.

The next day, my father implemented the next part of his plan. He changed the truck's insurance so my husband was the driver. If Dad couldn't make it not happen, and he couldn't even delay it, by gosh, he was in charge of stopping driving.

That's how the film I watched handled the wife's adjustment to the care facility. But in that fictional case, based on a story by Alice Munro, as she settled into the new place, she also forgot who her husband was, and fell in love with another patient. The transition was delicately played, as was the husband's effort to express his ongoing love and concern for someone who wasn't always able to remember the forty-five years of their marriage.

It's not a film I would recommend for everyone. It may strike too close to home for some people like my parents, who are guessing at a future in which any of us might play either lead role from that film. It certainly isn't likely to interest young adults like my friends and my grown kids, whose interest falters when the explosions/car chase/nudity ratio drops below par for modern films. But, there's a lot to enjoy in a film with a peripheral character who keeps a running hockey commentary going on everything happening around him: "As I approach the elevator, there's a man on my right with a broken heart. Broken into a thousand pieces. And the elevator doors open..."

So while I was enjoying winter sports this weekend, I watched our tracks fan out much like the skiing tracks did during the film. Even if my own kids are far away this winter, there's plenty of young people to relate to even though they're not my relations. It feels like the unsteady forgetfulness of the wife in the film, as she moves in a world where she gets on well with the people around her even when their names and roles escape her mental grasp. I'm not looking forward to making plans for my own future, and nobody likes to imagine diminished mental capacity. But to move in a world where people carefully get along, and treat each other well – that part wouldn't be too bad.

Hunting

My worldview changed on moving to the farm. There's plenty of space on an acreage, and not many people in it. Not humans anyways. Plenty of company if you count animals and birds.

But the bird population can be in the hundreds, if a flock comes by or rests in our windbreak trees while migrating. Falcons or hawks come by on windy days and hover over the chickenyard. They're obviously thinking of knocking off early from a hard day of peering around for field mice and voles, and just swinging on by that "take-out chicken place" in our yard. But it's better that they eat mice.

There are mice galore in the fields. We see their tracks and holes in the snow, and their trails in dry grass. In fall they find their way into farmhouses, looking for warm housing through the winter. In early spring they make another try, due to population pressures. I guess if I spent all winter in a burrow with my eleven brothers and sisters, I too would be looking for a place of my own come spring. That's the worldview of a mouse.

So we got used to the odd furry invader. It's not a big problem. We invested in traps, and some poison, but prefer the traps. For one thing, when the mouse is dead, it's dead right away, there in the trap. No worry that it's crawled off to die somewhere, only to be found later. And ugly as it may be to find a dead mouse in a trap on the floor, I find that easier than imagining said mouse dying slowly and horribly from poison. One whack! and it's all over. That has to be easier than being caught by a cat, but you just can't say that to some people. At least, not to people who have never had a mouse invasion and never had their worldview expand.

The cat was our third line of defence. It was actually the best one, since we didn't have to set her up with a spring catch, or find places to stash poison that the mice will get into but our young visitors wouldn't.

Alas, there was still the ugly problem of finding small dead animals around the house from time to time, but there doesn't seem to be any way of getting round that. Even when there are no small mouseholes, doors do occasionally get propped open in good weather. And, like the opportunists they are, mice will come in at any and every chance. Understanding that is part of how my worldview has changed.

So we learned how to block mouseholes, and set out traps, and praise the cat, but we don't really using poison. The first kind we bought was in pellet form, see, and when we put some out in an old bowl the cat managed to get at it. She ate rather a lot, too, before I took it away from her. It's no fun pouring ipecac or salt water down the cat's throat, and then guessing whether or not all of the pellets made it back out. So now we have hard bars of the mouse poison, and we stash it in nooks and crannies in the sheds, where the cat can't fit.

For the house, we relied more on the cat's regular patrols. She became an expert hunter, compared to the pampered city cat she used to be. My husband would pick her up from wherever she was sleeping (stretched out on the floor on warm days, curled up on the couch or a bed on cold days) and tell her "Pay the rent, cat, or I'll shave your butt and paint 'Coyote bait' on it and throw you outside." Then he would show her the mouse and it was game over.

We could tell that she would get bored in mid-winter and mid-summer, when there are fewer mice around. Playing with paper scraps and sharpening her claws on the walls got boring after a while. In summer, she went out and hunted pocket gophers.

This took considerably more effort than hunting mice, in some ways. Sure, the gophers are slower and are bigger targets than mice. But all it takes to escape a hunting cat is a quick dive down a gopher hole. She managed to catch pocket gophers from time to time, usually young ones, just settling down in their own tunnels. They weren't wise in the ways of the world yet – and that's how so many hawks and owls survive around here! – but they were of a considerable size compared to our slim cat. Finding their stilled forms laid out near the front porch, was a cue to admire the cat, showering her with praise and ear-rubbing.

How else can you reward a cat? My worldview never expanded to understanding cats, or our cat, all that well, and before I could complete my research our cat retired into graceful snoozing and drooling on a heating pad and fuzzy blanket. She has now gone to her happy hunting ground, if her dreams are any indicator of where she wanted to go. When sleeping, her paws would twitch and her ears and whiskers would swivel, as if she were tracking something. The world according to a cat is populated with opportunities. I like that worldview.

Memory

"I'm just having a senior moment," my mother said the other day. She waved a hand toward her computer. "I know I should be able to find things on the internet, but I just can't make it work. Getting my e-mail is okay. That I can do, just fine. But finding things on the internet? Nope."

That's a frustrating turn of events for her. Until she retired, she was a personnel clerk who kept the employment records straight for the Highways ministry, BC's largest government ministry. She assisted the systems analysts who designed the computer programs to keep the records, showing them what kind of data she needed to keep and how she wanted to access it. So when she finds it hard to learn how to use a word-processing program or Photoshop, or look something up on the internet, that is a difficult moment for her.

"It isn't Alzheimer's disease," she said with a wink. "It's just 'Old-timer's disease.'" She had a pamphlet describing the kinds of memory loss and function loss to worry about, the kinds that can be due to Alzheimer's disease or a brain injury or stroke. The pamphlet was actually very reassuring to her, as it also outlined several modest kinds of memory loss that are likely to happen once in a while for anyone, though perhaps a little more often with increasing age: misplacing keys, leaving a coffee cup somewhere, or being unwilling to admit to long-time friends exactly how you voted in the last few elections.

"I shouldn't call it 'having a senior moment,'" said my mother. "Apparently young people forget things all the time, too, but they don't get upset about it and worry they're going senile."

Still, severe memory problems are not that uncommon. As our population's average age increases, we'll be seeing more and more people diagnosed with Alzheimer's disease, in Canada and other countries. The latest famous person to announce that he or she has Alzheimer's disease is Terry Pratchett, author of several best-selling fantasy novels. I still don't know how the doctors figured out that he has the condition, when it's usually diagnosed after death, during an autopsy; but Pratchett is used to figuring out impossible things in his novels at least.

He doesn't seem to be able to imagine his way out of this story, though. He's been diagnosed with a rare early-onset form of the disease, called posterior cortical atrophy. That's a fancy term for "parts of the back of his brain are shrinking and shriveling." At fifty-nine, Pratchett is one of 15,000 people in the United Kingdom with early-onset dementia. He's starting to notice its effects on him in little ways, such as when he gets a sweater turned inside out, it's a bit of a puzzle to get it turned the right way round again. He also turned in his driver's licence because he didn't feel confident behind the wheel. Oddly enough, Pratchett can still write and is working on a new book, but typing is beyond him now.

Attending the Alzheimer's Research Trust annual conference, Prachett announced that to beat this disease, he is prepared to go to extreme lengths. It's not just that he's paying for his drug treatment because the National Health Service says he is too young to get it for free. "Personally, I'd eat the arse out of a dead mole if it offered a fighting chance," he said on the BBC. "I am, along with many others, scrabbling to stay ahead long enough to be there when the cure comes along. " He then donated a million dollars to their research fund.

Now, that's class.

Sometimes I wish that I had the confident strength that Pratchett still has, even while his brain is starting to fail him. I know I wish that my fiction writing had the confident strength of his novels. I'm writing a new book on health this season, about a different brain disorder, and that means doing a different kind of research than I've done before. But that's supposed to be good for my own brain, too, to be learning new facts and applying them in new ways. I'm having enough of what young people call "blonde moments" and older people call "senior moments" – and enough is enough. Time to keep doing brain exercises, to keep my brain cells agile and capable.

That's what my mother is doing, when she reads novels and does crossword puzzles with my father. She's trying to learn all the ins and outs of her computer's word processing program so that she can do the editing of a quarterly newsletter for their branch of the R.C. Legion. But it really is hard to figure out how to insert photographs and get the captions right, so usually my sister-in-law helps her get everything laid out neatly in time to print out the copies of the newsletter. It's a real collection of the more positive kinds of senior moments – award ceremonies, charitable donations, fund-raising events, and profiles of people just having fun. Whatever works.

Watching the Watchers

It's officially summer now, whatever the weather is doing and whatever the news is from various parts of the world. I can't get too worried about the news from far away, where vast things are moving in hidden ways towards unseen goals. And I can't let the changing weather here or anywhere keep me from enjoying the occasional good day that comes my way.

Part of summer here is an increased number of small boats on the water. Many of these are motorboats, out not just so that people can enjoy sunshine and waves and fresh air, but so people can watch whales. Yes, it was a paradox to enjoy Wild Nature from the deck of a powerboat howling along at a fuel-guzzling speed, but I got over it and enjoyed the ride.

Whale watching is big business. Most communities around the Strait of Georgia area have whale watching companies that take people out for a few hours. Tour guides point out the bobbing heads of seals and sea lions, and name a variety of birds from cormorants to eagles. For some tourists, seeing whales is the highlight of their visit. The guides all have two-way radios, and each day they try to find out where the whales are.

Some guides get a little too desperate to make sure their clients have a good sighting. That's where Straitwatch comes in. They're an organization that observes the whale watching boats, gathering data for the federal government on what really happens with whales and small boats. My partner Bernie and I volunteered to help Straitwatch collect data.

We met Kathy at 8:30 am at the Marina for an orientation. She fired up their 18-foot Zodiac. We zoomed over to Discovery Island – a trip that usually takes an hour or more in our kayaks – and hung out for a while, listening to radio reports. When her counterparts at Soundwatch, from Puget Sound , reported whale sightings near San Juan Island, we went there.

It turned out to be more than just one whale, or one family group called a pod. The superpod of J, K and L pods had gotten together for the equivalent of a big family barbecue. There were eighty to ninety whales, according to Kathy, and we saw several small groups. Some even approached the Zodiac to within 50 metres!

All day, we enjoyed seeing whales. There were usually eight to twelve small vessels nearby, watching whales, and most of the time the international rules about Not Approaching Whales were observed. I enjoyed seeing the opposite side of a very familiar two-humped hill on San Juan Island. These islands are like the ones in Canadian waters; that border is an intellectual line, not a physical one. Bernie did most of the data recording; I grinned and had a good time. It was a personal whale watching tour!

The most confusing moment was when a small steel-coloured boat came by, flying an American flag. "That's Homeland Security," said Kathy. We tried not to look like terrorists, but I'm not really sure what they were looking for. Vast things like government organizations are moving in hidden ways towards unseen goals, just as cryptic as the moving, singing whales in dark waters. Frankly, if whale watching or gathering data on whale watchers makes Homeland Security suspicious, well, we've all got to have more communication to ease those suspicions.

An hour of high-speed travel – the Zodiac has two engines that howled through over 80 litres of fuel – got us back to the Marina. Bernie and I saw a hummingbird, at the bus stop on our way to the Beach House. Next time we'll bike instead of bussing.

On The Beach

I find the darndest things when walking the dogs. No, I don't own any dogs. I have a time-share in my landlady's two dogs. Most time-shares are in interesting things like beachside cottages or luxury condo resorts. Not mine. The beach house is home, it's not a getaway cottage. It's as unlike a luxury condo resort as the dogs are unlike the retired racing whippet a neighbour walks daily past the beach house, driving the two dogs inside to barking frantically.

Barking is about all the dogs are good for, that and nosing around to find the darndest things in the beachside park. There's dog-slobbered tennis balls, Frisbees, and any number of discarded clothes of various sizes. Apparently people don't need to wear as many clothes going home from the beach as they wore on the way to get there. We even found a fender float my partner put aside for the sailboat he wants to own one day.

The beach park was busy last weekend, what with Sunday being SandFest with hundreds of families, a demonstration sandcastle, and almost enough vendors selling ice cream and Fresh! Squeezed! Lemonade! to rival an Edmonton-area festival. (How many Edmontonians does it take to change a light bulb? Ten thousand. One to change the bulb, and the other 9,999 to eat green onion cakes.) Saturday was a StrongMan Festival with the same vendors. And before that, Friday night was apparently Have Sex On The Beach Night for students from the university. They were stacked on the beach like driftwood when my partner and I went by while walking the dogs.

So we find the odd sandal or random piece of clothing. But five times in the past year, other people have found a sneaker with a foot in it on beaches among the Gulf Islands. Find a sneaker on the beach now and there's a tense moment as you turn the shoe over. Yup, whew, empty.

We talked about it once while on the water with friends in our kayaks. Among the words I never expected to use at the same time are "natural disarticulation." If you don't know what that means, you haven't seen the CBC reports on the feet in the sneakers. Eventually the police realized that "no sign of foul play" just wasn't enough explanation, and they explained that the feet had not been severed. Not that it's a comforting thought, but at least people stopped making wild guesses about criminal gangs removing feet for obscure and upsetting reasons.

And sure enough, one day our group saw something floating off-shore, about the size and colour and shape of a life jacket. We detoured to check it out. "Homemade crab trap float," reported Louise. "Whew! I thought it might be..."

Yeah, we all thought so. Turns out, we all knew what to do if we had found a floating body, as a family did in Portage Inlet last month, in exactly the spot where we found the jelly ball egg sacs last summer. Take a picture with camera or cell phone to show the authorities, if the body disappears. Use cell phone or VHF radio to call the authorities. And stay near the body, not touching it, until the authorities arrive. Might have got a bit tricky with the current coming up as the tide ebbs round Ten Mile Point... but that was all hypothetical, unlike the case in Portage Inlet. At least that dead man has been identified. And one of the mysterious feet in sneakers belongs to a man reported missing many months ago.

So far, all the footwear on our beach has been without feet, thank goodness. The dogs' big discovery after the party weekend was a kayak rudder and screwdriver in the beach park. That's the kind of odd thing I like them to find.

After the funeral

A long the fence line
of my back field this evening
I walk to the pile of stones
that Edouard Lutz picked.
He was born here, ninety-three years ago,
raised his own children in my little house.
He piled rocks here where the spring runoff
comes across the field in a wet year,
piled them to keep the land from wearing away
in a season of rushing water.
He worked as a boy with his father
then with his own sons.
He was a patient man.
I find the stones he left in piles along the fence lines.
They are patient, put there in time.
I walk out to the largest stone
with slim trees among the greatest pile,
deer tracks and wild roses.
I remember those who are mine who are gone
who gave me my few strengths
and this place.
And then I turn back,
my shadow stretching out
towards my little house
where he was born, and raised five children.
My shadow stretches out
over five acres, ten acres

the shadow of my head and moving hands
stretched out grand
so small across this wide land
under the broad sky.

Don't miss out!

Visit the website below and you can sign up to receive emails whenever Paula Johanson publishes a new book. There's no charge and no obligation.

https://books2read.com/r/B-A-ZKUK-IXJCC

BOOKS 2 READ

Connecting independent readers to independent writers.

Did you love *Under The Plow*? Then you should read *No Parent Is An Island*[1] by Paula Johanson!

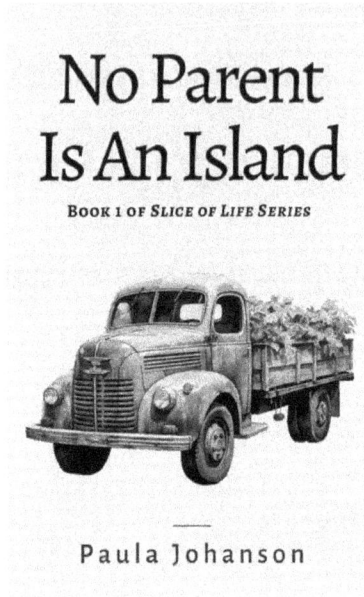

It's two a.m. and you've got a crying child and you know you'll never remember this five years from now, but tonight it's all there is.

It's two p.m. and the kids have covered themselves - outside and in! - with petroleum jelly, in just under thirty seconds. You know this could never happen to anyone else. Could it?

No Parent Is An Island explores those moments when life becomes ... an adventure! For author Paula Johanson, it has been an adventure complicated by twins, a farm, and a partner with an overdeveloped sense of humour. To say nothing of pigs, splendid isolation, and forgotten territory.

As Paula writes: *Sometimes all it takes is a single lyric, like the Travelling Willburys singing "I've been robbed and ridiculed/ in daycare centres and night schools/ handle me with care" to get people in daycare centres and night schools across a continent singing bits of a song, all that season, while rocking their kids.*

---

1. https://books2read.com/u/bxJGB6

2. https://books2read.com/u/bxJGB6

Doublejoy Books is pleased to present this new edition of *No Parent Is An Island*, a celebrated book that is now the first book in the *Slice of Life* series by Paula Johanson. Look for the sequel *Working Parent* with more family stories! The series goes on with *Under The Plow*, a collection of Johanson's popular op-ed columns for a rural newspaper.

"*Paula Johanson chronicles the adventure of parenthood with wry wit and ironic accuracy.*" - Jim Holland, editor, *Island Parent* magazine

"*I thoroughly enjoyed reading Paula's insight into parenting. I laughed (to tears) along with her at the antics of her children (and husband) and found myself nodding agreement over life's trials. Paula has found a way to survive with a smile. This book is a very pleasant reminder that children are fun, even when they challenge us to the Moon.*" - Christine Stusek, mother of three, artist, daycare provider

"*This book helped me stay sane when my kids were small. It's just the right size to keep in the bathroom.*" - eager fan who bought two more autographed copies to give her friends.

Read more at books2read.com/paulaj.

Also by Paula Johanson

Alt-Academic
Woolgathering: Awareness of the Foreign in Published Works About
Cowichan Woolworking
Sanitizer

Prime Ministers of Canada
Pierre Elliott Trudeau: Child of Nature
Charles Tupper: Warhorse

Slice of Life
No Parent Is An Island
Working Parent
Under The Plow

Young Science
Bat Poop Sparkles
Otters Hold Hands

Standalone

Small Rain and Other Nightmares
Island Views
Plum Tree
Tower in the Crooked Wood
King Kwong: Larry Kwong, the China Clipper Who Broke the NHL Colour
Barrier
Science Critters
Green Paddler

About the Author

Paula Johanson is a Canadian writer. A graduate of the University of Victoria with an MA in Canadian literature, she has worked as a security guard, a short order cook, a teacher, newspaper writer, and more. As well as editing books and teaching materials, she has run an organic-method small farm with her spouse, raised gifted twins, and cleaned university dormitories. In addition to novels and stories, she is the author of forty-two books written for educational publishers, among them *The Paleolithic Revolution* and *Women Writers* from the series *Defying Convention: Women Who Changed The World*. Johanson is an active member of SF Canada, the national association of science fiction and fantasy authors.

Read more at books2read.com/paulaj.

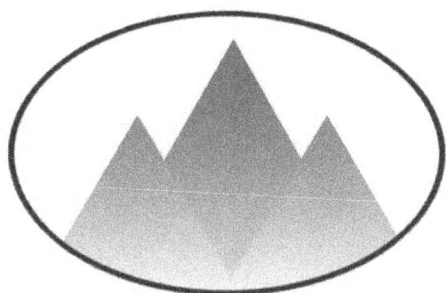

Doublejoy Books

About the Publisher

Doublejoy Books is the publisher of a variety of eclectic books of Canadian literature.

http://doublejoybooks.com
http://books2read.com/paulaj

www.ingramcontent.com/pod-product-compliance
Lightning Source LLC
LaVergne TN
LVHW091254080426
835510LV00007B/264